THE BEST IS YET TO BE

THE BEST IS YET TO BE

LEROY PATTERSON

Tyndale House Publishers, Inc.
Wheaton, Illinois

All Scripture is taken from *The Living Bible* unless otherwise noted.

Scripture quotations identified RSV are from the *Revised Standard Version* and are used by permission of the Division of Christian Education of the National Council of the Churches of Christ in the U.S.A.

Scripture quotations from *The New Testament in Modern English* (by J.B. Phillips) are used by permission of Macmillan Publishing Co., Inc.

Scripture quotations identified NIV are from the *New International Version* and are used by permission of the New York International Bible Society.

Poem, "He Giveth More" taken from the book, *BUT GOD* by Annie Johnson Flint, Scripture Press Publications, Ltd. Toronto, Canada. Used by permission.

First printing, March 1986

Library of Congress Catalog Card Number 85-52011
ISBN 0-8423-0183-6
Copyright 1986 by LeRoy Patterson
All rights reserved
Printed in the United States of America

*Dedicated to the memory of my father,
who enjoyed retirement and never looked back.*

*And to my ninety-year-old mother
whose love and devotion have prompted the writing of
this book.*

C O N T E N T S

BOOKS WORTH READING...

PREFACE

AGE is relative.

To a six-year-old, a teenager is old.

To a teenager, anyone over thirty is much too old.

And to a thirty-year-old, anyone who has reached retirement age has earned the right to be canonized.

This view of aging was dramatically illustrated at a family reunion when a six-year-old boy shocked the family by asking his grandfather, "Were you in Noah's ark?"

Fortunately, Grandpa laughed along with the rest and replied, "No, grandson, I missed the ark."

That should have settled it, but the little fellow came back with, "Then why didn't you drown?" At least he knew the Bible story.

In spite of the misperception of the young, growing older is a rewarding fact of life to anticipate with delight, not dread. The poet who wrote, "Grow old along with me, the best is yet to be," was not merely expressing a sentimental thought. The best is truly yet to be for the trusting Christian. To walk with God in the autumn of life is a time of discovery and delight.

These brief, devotional thoughts are designed to remind us of the grace and mercy of our loving Lord, who promised, "Be sure of this, that I am with you always, even to the end of the world" (Matt. 28:20).

**I WILL MEDITATE ON ALL THY WORK,
AND MUSE ON ALL THY MIGHTY DEEDS.**
Psalm 77:12 (RSV)

MEDITATIONS

ATTITUDES

THE ONE THING I WANT FROM GOD, THE THING I SEEK MOST OF ALL, IS . . . LIVING IN HIS PRESENCE EVERY DAY OF MY LIFE, DELIGHTING IN HIS INCOMPARABLE PERFECTIONS AND GLORY. Psalm 27:4

THE JOY OF THE LORD

I have told you this so that you will be filled with my joy. Yes, your cup of joy will overflow!
John 15:11

OF all the people in the world, the Christian is the one who has the right to be most joyful. We have been forgiven, restored, cleansed, and made whole. We are the recipients of God's many promises, and have been included as members of his very own family. We have been given a hope that transcends our brief stay upon the earth, and the promise of an eternal life with Christ, free from the ravages of sin, disease, sorrow, and death. What more do we need to make us happy?

Yet, in spite of these innumerable blessings, we often seem to lack that deep consistent note of joy. This is probably due to our misunderstanding of the nature of joy. It is a common fallacy to believe that true joy is dependent upon our economic status, our physical health, or the absence of any suffering. Yet Jesus faced disappointment, poverty, physical suffering, and sorrow, without losing that inner joy. And the remarkable thing is, he has promised that you and I can be filled with his own joy. John 15:11 promises, "You will be filled with *my* joy." The joy that Jesus experienced sustained him through difficult and trying situations. It remained with him even as he "was willing to die a shameful death on the cross because of the joy he knew would be his afterwards" (Heb. 12:2).

This, then, is the kind of joy that we can all experience. And how do we get it? The answer is given by Jesus in John 16:24, "Ask, using my name . . . and your cup of joy will overflow." This is so elementary that we find it difficult to do.

If Jesus had asked us to attend a ten-day conference on joy, or listen to a series of tapes, or even enroll in a course on the subject at a Christian college, we would have gladly complied. But when he simply requests us to "Ask, using my name," we often fail to follow his request.

Let us rejoice, then, heeding the advice of Paul, who wrote, "Always be full of joy in the Lord; I say it again, rejoice!" (Phil. 4:4).

Prayer

Dear Father, in the strong name of Jesus my Lord, I ask you to fill me with his joy. Whenever I am despondent, or filled with sadness, or just physically and emotionally spent, lift my spirit and "restore unto me the joy of my salvation." Amen.

TRUST, COMMITMENT, AND REST

Commit everything you do to the Lord. Trust him to help you do it and he will. Psalm 37:5

THREE words stand out in the first seven verses of Psalm 37. They are: trust, commit, and rest. Psalm 37:3 says, "Trust in the Lord . . ."; verse 5 adds, "Commit everything you do to the Lord . . ." and verse 7 admonishes, "Rest in the Lord. . . ." There is a beautiful spiritual progression in the order of these three verbs.

My mother was in her late seventies before she had her first airplane ride. It took a great deal of coaxing and persuading, but she finally agreed to make the trip from Boston to Chicago. It was also my father's first time in the air, but he was relaxed about the whole thing. In fact, when my mother was too nervous to eat the meal served on the plane, Dad gallantly ate hers as well as his own.

Having done considerable flying myself, both as a passenger and as a private pilot, I gave my mother some sound advice just before her plane took off. I said, "Mom, you have indicated your trust in the airlines by purchasing your ticket, and now that you have boarded the plane, you have committed yourself to this trip. So just lean back in your seat and rest— enjoy the ride."

I didn't realize it at the time, but that is a perfect prescription for one who wants to be free of worry. Trust, commitment, and rest represent the three steps to a life of peace and well-being.

Buying the ticket was the first indication of faith. It represented a trust in the carrier. Walking out and boarding the plane was the second step, and that revealed a commitment. But if a person is to be really worry free, there must be more than trust and commitment. There must also be rest. That means the ability to relax, lean back in the seat, and enjoy the trip. It's no fun to fly for hours, gripping the armrests with white knuckles.

Whether or not we enjoy our journey of faith with the Lord depends on what we do with the active verbs, trust, commit, and rest.

Will we lean back and rest in the Lord—or worry?

Let's enjoy the journey.

Prayer

Lord, you have promised to bear me up on eagle's wings. I confess that at times I forget who it is who is bearing me up. Strengthen my trust in you. Help me to learn how to truly commit my way to you— and rest. Amen.

 # PONDERING THE IMPONDERABLES

There are secrets the Lord your God has not revealed to us, but these words which he has revealed are for us and our children to obey forever. Deuteronomy 29:29

THE talk show host was interviewing a man who had reached his hundredth birthday. He asked him the usual question, "To what do you attribute your longevity?" Without a moment's hesitation the old gentleman replied, "A long time ago I learned not to ponder the imponderable and unscrew the inscrutable." He went on to explain that many people shorten their lives by worrying about things that have no answer.

When I heard him say this, I immediately thought of a verse of Scripture I learned early in my Christian life, "There are secrets the Lord your God has not revealed to us, but these words which he has revealed are for us and our children to obey forever" (Deut. 29:29).

Moses was instructing the people of Israel that, although there were secrets God had not revealed, they should be more concerned with the things God had shown them. There is much wisdom in Moses' words for us. The person who is constantly asking God *why?* usually becomes quite upset and frustrated. How often have we heard, "Why do the righteous suffer while the unrighteous seem to prosper?"

"Why does God allow war, poverty and discrimination to exist?"

"Why does the drunk driver survive the accident, while an entire family is wiped out?"

Life seems full of mysteries and contradictions.

The Christian who is able to avoid "pondering the imponderables, and unscrewing the inscrutable" is usually a much more peaceful Christian. There comes a time when we must commit the "secret things" to the Lord, and to trust in his justice. When Abraham was confronted with such a situation, he simply said, "Will not the Judge of all the earth be fair?" That settled it for Abraham. Whatever God decreed, or allowed, had to be just, for he is the God of perfect justice.

The next time you are tempted to brood over questions that have no answers, take Moses' and Abraham's advice. Leave the secret things with God, and begin to concentrate on the things which he has revealed. Who knows, you too might live to be a hundred!

Prayer

Lord, you have told us that "your ways are not our ways." Give us the faith to believe that you are right and just in all your ways, and to trust you, even in the situations we do not understand. Amen.

 WHY PRAY WHEN YOU CAN WORRY?

Don't worry about anything; instead, pray about everything; tell God your needs and don't forget to thank him for his answers. If you do this you will experience God's peace. Philippians 4:6, 7

WHILE driving through Chicago one day, my vision was partially obscured by the black exhaust pouring from a dilapidated VW. As I passed this moving wreck, I saw a bumper sticker on the rear which read, "Why pray when you can worry?" The young driver gave me a broad smile and a wave as I passed, as if to say, "I haven't a worry in the world." The bumper sticker was obviously tongue-in-cheek, but it aptly described the philosophy of all too many Christians. However, we need to distinguish between concern and worry. Concern is a momentary apprehension, while worry is a preoccupation with concerns. For example, if a child is playing on the sidewalk, and the mother hears a loud squealing of brakes, it is perfectly normal to feel a sudden tug of fear. But if this same mother were to sit by the window, constantly watching her child, that is worry—overwhelming anxiety.

In the above text Paul is speaking about preoccupation with concerns, and he says bluntly, "Don't worry about anything." There are several practical reasons for this admonition. For one thing, worry can immobilize us mentally, physically, emotionally, and spiritually. It is a proven fact that many of our physical ailments are caused by excessive anxiety. There is an epitaph on an old tombstone that was probably prophetic. It reads, "Here lies the body of Josiah Quick, who departed this life, worried sick."

Worry also reflects upon the trustworthiness of God. It says God has promised to provide for *all* my needs, but I don't really believe it. Thus we are calling God's credibility to account. Furthermore, worry has no ability to alter any situation. Jesus said, "Don't worry . . ." and then he asked, "Will all your worries add a single moment to your life?" (Matt. 6:25-34).

Paul's remedy for worry sounds almost too simplistic, but it is the only one that really works. "Tell God your needs, and don't forget to thank him for his answers." The old gospel song, "Take your burdens to the Lord and leave them there," might sound impractical to our enlightened generation, but it is biblically sound.

What action will you take in dealing with anxiety? Will it be "Why pray when you can worry?" or, "Why worry when you can pray?"

Prayer
Father, if even the birds have sense enough not to worry, I promise to trust you to provide for every need. And remind me to talk with you about my concerns. Amen.

A CURE FOR IRRITATIONS

Hillsides blossom with joy. The pastures are filled with flocks of sheep, and the valleys are carpeted with grain. All the world shouts with joy, and sings. Psalm 65:12, 13

THE other morning when reading Psalm 65, I remembered an incident that was related to me a few years ago. George and Ruth looked forward for years to retirement in the country. Every weekend they had driven over the back roads to various farms, looking for the ideal location. Finally they settled upon a vacant farmhouse located in central Pennsylvania. It was on the side of a hill, overlooking a lush meadow. A small, clear trout stream wound its way through the pasture like a silver thread. This was the fulfillment of their lifetime dream.

They moved in and for a time were deliriously happy. But then Ruth began to show signs of restlessness. She complained of nervousness, and the doctor gave her a mild tranquilizer, but her condition didn't improve.

Then one day while they were having their morning coffee, one of the neighbor ladies dropped in. She was an elderly woman who lived alone, and had learned a lot about contentment. As Ruth shared her problem with her, her neighbor began to smile. "You don't need a doctor," she said, "you need a carpenter." "What in the world for?" Ruth asked. The elderly lady responded, "Tell him you want a large picture window installed in that blank wall in the kitchen."

It seemed like an odd prescription, but George and Ruth decided to have the window installed. Day after day, as Ruth stood by the sink, her eyes drank in the beauty and tranquility of God's lovely meadows. She saw the cows grazing contentedly in the fields, and the beauty of the sky as the sun set each evening behind the hills. She watched the rain clouds come and go. Within a matter of weeks her "irritations" ceased, and she was her normal, contented self.

The next time you are feeling hemmed in, and the problems of life appear like a blank wall, take a drive out into the countryside. Like David, "Lift up your eyes to the hills," and see "the valleys . . . carpeted with grain." Then quietly look up into the face of God and make a complete submission of your life to the Lord. You will be surprised at the peace God will bring into your soul. It is better than a ton of tranquilizers.

Prayer
Lord Jesus, you have promised to let your peace flow out to me. I pray that you will fill me with your gracious Spirit, and calm my troubled heart. I yield myself anew to your loving control. Amen.

 # GIVING THANKS FOR EVERYTHING

Always be thankful, for this is God's will for you who belong to Christ Jesus. 1 Thessalonians 5:18

DR. Alexander Whyte of Edinburgh was famous for his pulpit prayers. People joked about the fact that he was able to find some good in almost everything that happened. One miserably cold rainy Sunday morning he opened the service by praying, "We thank thee, O God, that it is not always like this!" It was one of the few times that quiet snickers were heard in that staid, old church sanctuary.

C.S. Lewis, noted British author and lecturer, cited an original parable to bring out a truth about human gratitude, and the lack of it. He told of two groups of people on a tour. The one group had been promised that they would be housed at a luxury hotel, while the other group was told they would be staying at a local prison. But instead, both groups were housed in very modest homes.

Consequently, the ones who had been promised the best, complained the most. They groused that there was no heat, the beds were lumpy, the food was mediocre, and the tea was cold. On the other hand, those who had been promised the least were ecstatic with joy. They thanked God for their accommodations, for having a bed to sleep in, rather than a mat, and for food that was far better than they had expected.

What was the difference? It was in the promise. Lewis's point was that God has not promised us an easy life. He never promised us freedom from sickness, sorrow or suffering. Therefore, when unpleasant things occur, we can say with Dr. Whyte, "We thank thee, O God, that it is not always like this!"

Paul was one who practiced what he preached. He not only admonished us to always be thankful, but he said of himself, "I have learned to get along happily whether I have much or little. I have learned to live on almost nothing, or with everything."

It is only when we can face life with that kind of attitude that we can say, "I will be thankful in *all* circumstances."

Prayer
Dear Lord, help me to be more grateful for all the blessings you bring into my life. Yes, even to be grateful for some of the unpleasant things that happen from time to time. It makes me appreciate the good things even more. Amen.

WHAT MAKES YOU HAPPY?

But happy is the man who has the God of Jacob as his helper, whose hope is in the Lord his God. Psalm 146:5

THERE are a lot of unhappy people in the world. This has led many people to become quite cynical. An older man who had been an atheist all his life, wrote, "The promise of happiness is a monumental fraud." An aging movie star, in a recent interview for a national magazine, said, "Happiness is a cruel illusion, which can only taunt and mislead us all."

Obviously, both the atheist and the movie star had failed to find the secret of true happiness, which is found only in the living God, and which is transmitted through him to every believer.

There are a number of myths about the subject. Some think that happiness is merely a matter of comparisons. They say, "I can be happy if I am richer than others," or more popular, or stronger, or more intelligent. In other words, their happiness depends upon how well they measure up to their peers.

Another myth about happiness is that it can result from a change of circumstances. There are those who believe that if they could only change jobs, or move to a new area of the country, or find a new wife or husband, they would find true happiness. Sometimes a change of circumstance will make us happy for a time, but there has to be a deeper and more permanent solution.

The verse from this Psalm would seem to indicate that true happiness is impossible unless it is rooted in God. No amount of money, new jobs, new spouses, or new surroundings can compensate for a life without the Lord. Such a life is shallow, empty, and full of unhappiness.

What makes you happy? Your answer to that key question will tell a great deal about you, your values, your goals, and your faith. Remember—"Happy is *that* man whose hope is in the Lord."

Prayer

Father, you want your children to be happy. Forgive my shortsightedness in failing to see that there is no lasting happiness apart from you. Help me to share this great truth with the many people around me who are so miserably unhappy. Amen.

THE SECRET OF CONTENTMENT

I have learned how to get along happily whether I have much or little. I know how to live on almost nothing or with everything. I have learned the secret of contentment in every situation.
Philippians 4:11, 12

WE are told that contentment is the result of freedom from responsibility. Television ads picture the retired couple lying on a beach, watching the tide roll in, with happy smiles on their faces. The implication is that contentment can be found simply by retiring. Any retired person, however, can testify to the fallacy of this concept.

I have a friend who pastors a church in Florida that has a large number of retirees. After he had been there a short time he told me, "There is more grumpiness per square foot of pew here than anywhere I've ever been." Obviously, retirement is not a cure-all for discontent.

In Paul's beautiful thank-you note to the Philippian believers for their sacrificial gifts, he indicated that contentment is a quality that comes only through yielding to the sovereign will of God. Twice in this note he said, "I have learned" to be content.

Contentment is not something that is conferred upon us at conversion or confirmation, or even retirement. It is a quality of life that must be learned.

The wording of the text indicates that Paul himself had not always possessed the desirable state of mind called contentment, but somehow through the experiences of life he had mastered its elusive secret.

We must learn the secret also. Most of us grew up thinking that contentment was something that came with the accumulation of things. How devastatingly destructive that idea is. According to the Apostle Paul, true contentment comes only with a total trust in the Lord. This truth is expressed in the words of an older man who paraphrased the Twenty-third Psalm: "The Lord is my Shepherd, I have everything that I need!"

Prayer
Dear Father, your Word assures me that "it is he who will supply all my needs from his riches in glory." Help me to be content with my situation in life, knowing that you will be faithful in meeting all of my needs. Amen.

 # COPING WITH LONELINESS

He [Jacob] . . . then returned again to the camp and was there alone; and a Man wrestled with him until dawn. Genesis 32:24

JACOB'S midnight wrestling with God is a familiar story. His entire life, up to this point, had been characterized by fraud and deceit. He had deceived his brother, his parents, and his uncle Laban. But his string had run out, and God had backed him into a corner, alone. He experienced the loneliness of isolation.

Another form of loneliness is called alienation. This is the loneliness of those who have been excluded from the fellowship of others. It happens in neighborhoods, schools, social clubs, and even in churches.

Then there is a loneliness of separation. It can be a separation caused by divorce, death, or simply watching our children leave home to begin a life of their own. No matter the reason, it is always quite painful.

But loneliness at the very deepest level is what has been called an existential loneliness. This is the loneliness experienced by those who have no personal relationship with God. They exist, but with no real purpose or meaning. When they are stripped of every other support, like Jacob, they are left alone.

We all experience one or more of these forms of loneliness. But as we face retirement, we must live with a new kind of loneliness. We miss our friends at the office or plant. Our children have married, and have children of their own. Many of our friends have retired and moved away, and there is an emptiness that was not evident before. And unless we have prepared ourselves for this, we can feel devastated and lost.

Fortunately, we do not need to be defeated by loneliness. We can make new friends and become involved in the lives of others. We can become active in a church and offer our talents and abilities to further the work of the kingdom. We can find opportunities for civic service and volunteer for organizations. Our lives can take on a newer and deeper dimension. Our loneliness can become a creative channel of God's blessing.

Jacob's story has a happy ending. He was brought to a place of submission to God, and his life was transformed. He was given a new start, a new name, a new character, and a new hope. His loneliness was swallowed up in victory. It can happen to any of us.

Prayer
Lord, in those times of loneliness, I pray that you will bless me as you did Jacob and fill my life with yourself. Amen.

THE DROOPING HEAD SYNDROME

Lord, you are my shield, my glory, and my only hope. You alone can lift my head. Psalm 3:3

HAVE you ever noticed how few people walk with their heads held high? The next time you are in a crowd, take a look around and you will be surprised at the great number of people who suffer from the drooping head. The reasons for this vary.

For some it is caused by some deep sorrow. This was true of the Psalmist, who had lived to see his beloved son Absalom betray him, and as a consequence, his son had been executed. The heading of Psalm 3 reads, *"A Psalm of David when he fled from his son Absalom."* That tells the whole tragic story. David's head was bowed down with grief and sorrow. This is also true of many people in the world.

Sometimes the head can be bowed down because of the weight of some physical infirmity. It is difficult to be sunny and cheerful when we are hurting physically. Perhaps you are one of those who have had to suffer a great deal of physical infirmity. As we grow older, pain often is our companion.

For many the head is bowed because of a sense of failure. My football coach in college was somewhat of an amateur psychologist. When any of us would fumble the ball, or miss a tackle, and our heads would drop in shame, we would hear that booming voice from the sidelines shouting, "Get your chin up!" Nothing will cause discouragement more readily than a sense of failure.

Occasionally the bowed head is due to a sense of guilt because of our sins. Many a Christian has been brought low with humiliation and guilt because of some sin. The good news of the gospel is that Jesus has forgiven us every transgression.

David said, "You alone, Lord, can lift up my head." The Lord may do this by changing the circumstances that first caused the head to droop. But more often he chooses to lift the drooping head, not by removing the problem, but by giving us the strength and ability to cope with it. God wants to help us, as he did David, not necessarily by removing our "thorns," but by giving us the grace to deal with them and be victorious. And in this way, like David, we can say, "Lord, you alone can lift up my head."

Prayer
   Blessed Lord, in thee is refuge,
   Safety for my trembling soul;
   Power to lift my head when drooping,
   While the angry billows roll. Amen.

GETTING A NEW GRIP ON OURSELVES

So take a new grip with your tired hands, stand firm on your shaky legs, and mark out a straight, smooth path for your feet. Hebrews 12:12, 13

THERE is the sound of battle in these words; there is the clash of opposing forces, the struggle of athletic bodies, the evidences of tiring hands and legs, and the staggering of weakened feet. It sounds like a normal Sunday afternoon of mayhem in the professional football leagues. It has been said that professional football is a game where seventy-five-thousand fans who desperately need exercise are cheering for twenty-two tired athletes who desperately need rest.

Such a scene is found in the twelfth chapter of Hebrews. A huge stadium is filled with cheering spectators, and only a handful of participants. The athletes are pictured stripping off their outer warm-up garments and straining to reach the finish line. As the race progresses, arms become weary, legs begin to tremble with weakness, and the runner has all he or she can do to keep from straying out of the lane.

It is at this point that the runner needs to get a "second wind," a fresh infusion of physical and mental toughness in order to finish the race. Or, as the Scripture exhorts, "Take a new grip."

This athletic illustration has a spiritual application for those of us who have been in this race for a longer time. Living the Christian life requires discipline, endurance, correction, and a lot of practice. It is not easy. We are competing against powerful opponents. But we have God's promise that the Holy Spirit, who is more powerful than all the forces arrayed against us, will be with us.

Then when our spiritual arms and legs become tired and begin to tremble, we will be able to get a new grip on ourselves and continue on with the Holy Spirit's help.

Prayer
Dear Lord, I never get tired *of* your service, but I frequently grow tired *in* your service. Strengthen me by your Spirit so that I might serve you effectively, until the race is won. Amen.

INSEPARABLE LOVE

Nothing will ever be able to separate us from the love of God demonstrated by our Lord Jesus Christ when he died for us. Romans 8:39

A friend of mine asked me to visit his aged mother who was in a rest home in a Chicago suburb. He explained that she had been exceptionally depressed and uncommunicative recently. Since this was contrary to her usual cheerful attitude, he was concerned.

After talking with my friend's mother for a while, she confided that she was concerned that God no longer loved her. Of course, that is not unusual for older Christians who have been alone a great deal. As I read "Nothing will ever be able to separate us from the love of God" and prayed with her, I could sense a new spirit of hope and confidence.

Our love for God may waver, and often does, for it is subject to changing moods and circumstances. But God's love for us is constant. Nothing in this great universe can separate us from that!

Then, just to make sure that we grasp this great truth, the Apostle Paul twice says, *"Nothing* can ever separate us from [God's] love" (Rom. 8:38, 39). And to further emphasize this fact, he lists some possible enemies that might attempt to sever us from God's love. He mentions "trouble, calamity, poverty, danger and hunger," and even these awful physical afflictions, we are told, are powerless to disprove God's love.

And just as physical afflictions are unable to sever us from God, neither can spiritual powers. "All the powers of hell itself cannot keep God's love away" (Rom. 8:38). The Devil is powerful, but he is not all-powerful. He is utterly helpless to snatch any of God's children from him.

Furthermore, neither time nor space, neither height nor depth can diminish that love.

> The love of God is greater far
>   Than tongue or pen can ever tell;
> It goes beyond the highest star,
>   And reaches to the lowest hell.

Finally, just in case he might have overlooked some possibility, Paul adds, "Nothing [in all creation] will ever be able to separate us from the love of God." That is about as exhaustive as anything can be.

> From him who loves me now so well,
> No power my soul can sever;
> Shall life or death, or earth or hell?
> No, I am his forever!

Prayer
Thank you, Lord, for your everlasting love. Amen.

 # YOU ARE NEEDED

And now, in my old age, don't set me aside. Don't forsake me now when my strength is failing. Psalm 71:9

"I hate this feeling of not being needed," said my seventy-two-year-old neighbor as we stood talking. I knew what he meant. Many of us who in the past filled places of responsibility in our families, in our communities, in business and in our churches no longer feel needed. Like David, we cry out, "Now, in my old age, don't set me aside."

I don't think David was indulging in self-pity. Rather, he was facing one of the realities of being older. He had lived a full and vigorous life. In earlier years his growing family depended on his strength. The entire nation of Israel had looked to him for leadership. Now he recognized he was no longer needed in the same ways by his family or by his nation. And so he cried out asking God not to cast him off like a worn-out sandal.

Retirement years are better years when we face realities head-on and talk with God about our feelings and the changes in our lives. True, businesses we once managed now thrive under new management. The churches we served faithfully carry on and grow.

Even our families seem to have little need for our day by day help.

But seeing responsibilities we once held successfully taken over by others, means that we did our jobs well, laid good foundations. Let us thank God we were able to help others mature and equip them to carry on independently.

Let us also thank him for today and trust him to make us aware of the people in our lives who need us now. People of all ages need each other—and need to be needed. During retirement, Christian fellowship and service are essential. And as long as we are sensitive to the needs of those around us we will be needed.

Prayer
Loving Father, there are so many adjustments to be made in this new life of retirement. And there are so many needy people all around me. Help me to look beyond my own needs, and to seek out those who need me. Let me be able to share the love and compassion of Jesus with the many new people I am meeting. Amen.

POCKETS WITH HOLES

You plant much but harvest little. You have scarcely enough to eat or drink, and not enough clothes to keep you warm. Your income disappears, as though you were putting it into pockets filled with holes! Haggai 1:6

IN my first pastorate in rural New Hampshire I met a seventy-nine-year-old hermit who fitted the above description perfectly. He lived in a miserable shack on the edge of the village and was shunned by all. His clothing was inadequate—mismatched castoffs, and his one-room house was a disaster. However, I learned that he had graduated from a prestigious eastern medical school and had practiced medicine for a number of years. But due to an addiction to alcohol, he had lost his lucrative practice, his family, and his self-respect. Now he was living out his remaining years as a hopeless recluse. His former house, property, and investments had long since disappeared. He was totally without friends and without God.

"Think it over," says the Lord of Hosts. "Consider how you have acted, and what has happened as a result!" (Hag. 1:7). The thrust of Haggai's message to Israel was that life without the Lord is a totally disappointing and unproductive life. Even though the Israelites had sowed much, they had harvested little. The summer of their life was almost over, and they had nothing to show for it. Furthermore, their life was unfulfilling. They had eaten and drunk, but were never full. They had dressed themselves in clothing that could not keep out the cold of winter.

In addition to that, their life was unrewarding. They had put their wages into their pockets, only to discover that the pockets were full of holes. What a disappointment! Probably we have all had such an experience at one time or another.

This is a most graphic picture of the emptiness of a life without God. Unproductive harvests, inadequate sustenance, unprotective clothing and shelter, and disappearing investments! This is a summary of the life story of multitudes of people.

On the other hand, as Christians, we have been assured that whatever we have invested of our resources, time or service with the Lord is productive. The Bible promises, "Your labor is not in vain in the Lord." That's one way to plug the holes in our pockets.

Prayer
Heavenly Father, I pray that my life will be fruitful and fulfilling. I do not want to invest the resources you have given me in unworthy ways. Give me the wisdom to distinguish between the temporal and the eternal, so that I might make a wise investment of my life. Amen.

WHY ME, LORD?

For to you has been given the privilege not only of trusting him but also of suffering for him.
Philippians 1:29

GOOD people never suffer—that ancient idea is still alive and well. We hear it from radio and television preachers, and occasionally from some church pulpits. This popular philosophy reasons that a good God would never allow righteous people to suffer, and a just God would never permit the unrighteous to go unpunished.

On the surface that reasoning makes a lot of common sense. But it completely ignores the realities of life, as well as the truth of Scripture. It wrongly assumes that nothing good can come from suffering, thus ignoring the plain teaching of the Bible. According to the writers of sacred Scripture there are some very positive results of suffering.

For one thing, the Bible tells us that suffering has a way of deepening and developing patience. Paul writes, "We can rejoice . . . when we run into problems and trials for we know that they are good for us—they help us learn to be patient" (Rom. 5:3, 4). This is the same word used in Hebrews 12:1, "Let us run with patience."

Patience implies "endurance." This is why athletes subject their bodies to the long, arduous, grueling hours of calisthenics. They patiently endure suffering today, so that they will have endurance for the race tomorrow. The Christian who has learned the discipline of suffering will not likely be a dropout.

Scripture also tells us that suffering produces character (see Jas. 1:2-4). Some of the strongest Christian characters I have known have been people who have endured considerable suffering.

Paul also informs us that suffering equips us to minister more effectively to a suffering society. "Our Lord Jesus Christ . . . the one who so wonderfully comforts and strengthens us in our hardships and trials. And why does he do this? So that when others are troubled, needing our sympathy and encouragement, we can pass on to them this same help and comfort God has given us" (2 Cor. 1:3, 4). It is only by enduring suffering ourselves that we can fully identify with the suffering of others and minister God's comfort.

Prayer
Dear Father, thank you for disciplining me in love. Without it I would be weak and incapable of enduring the sufferings of life. And without it, I would be unable to comfort others who are in deep distress. Amen.

M u s i n g s . . .

When saving for old age, be sure to put away a few pleasant thoughts. Author Unknown

If you have no joy in your religion, there's a leak in your Christianity somewhere.
W.A. (Billy) Sunday

Jesus promised his people three things—that they would be in constant trouble, completely fearless, and absurdly happy. Russel Maltby

Two men looked out of the prison bars;
The one saw mud; the other stars.
An old rhyme.

We can't solve problems for others, but we can introduce them to the Lord. Corrie ten Boom

I long to accomplish a great and noble task, but it is my chief and noble duty to accomplish tasks as though they were great and noble.

The world is moved along, not only by the mighty shoves of its heroes, but also by the aggregate of the tiny pushes of each honest worker. Helen Keller

> *It was only a glad "Good Morning"*
> *As she passed along the way,*
> *But it spread the morning's glory*
> *Over the livelong day.*
> Charlotte Augusta Perry
> *Good Morning*

Pain is inevitable. Suffering is optional.
Kathleen Casey Theisen

So this is now the mark by which we all shall certainly know whether the birth of the Lord Jesus is effective in us: if we take upon ourselves the needs of our neighbor. Martin Luther

Always be full of joy in the Lord . . . rejoice! Don't worry about anything; instead, pray about everything; tell God your needs . . . thank him for his answers. Philippians 4:4–6

Now your attitudes and thoughts must all be constantly changing for the better. Ephesians 4:23

Delight thyself also in the Lord; and he shall give thee the desires of thine heart. Psalm 37:4 (KJV)

MEDITATIONS

LIFESTYLE

OH, THE JOYS OF THOSE WHO ...
DELIGHT IN DOING EVERYTHING
GOD WANTS THEM TO, AND DAY
AND NIGHT ARE ALWAYS MEDI-
TATING ON HIS LAWS AND THINK-
ING ABOUT WAYS TO FOLLOW HIM
MORE CLOSELY. Psalm 1:1, 2

# COATS, BOOKS, AND PARCHMENTS

When you come, be sure to bring the coat I left at Troas with Brother Carpus, and also the books, but especially the parchments. 2 Timothy 4:13

AT the time of Paul's request to young Timothy he was nearing the end of his pilgrimage, and was imprisoned in a strange country. I have often wondered if I had been in his shoes and had made three last requests, what would they be? I would certainly not ask for money, for that would be useless. A new house and furniture would not meet my most pressing needs. Neither would a drawer full of stocks and bonds be any comfort.

Notice what Paul's requests were: first, he longed to have his old familiar coat. He had left it with young Carpus when he had fled Troas in haste. That comfortable old garment had kept out the chill of many a winter, and shielded him from the cold, wet ocean spray. Next, Paul requested that Timothy bring his favorite books. These probably included his favorite classics, copies of Roman law and history, and possibly some of the writings of the great poets and philosophers of his time. His third and final request was for the "parchments." Most biblical commentators believe these to be copies of some of the sacred rolls of Scripture, and perhaps some of his own writings.

It is interesting to observe that in Paul's three requests we have represented the three basic needs of humanity. The coat represented the needs of the body, the books provide for the needs of the mind, and the parchments, the Word of God, stand for the needs of the spirit.

In preparing for retirement, my wife and I knew that we would have to get rid of much that we had accumulated over the years. A lot of our clothing went into the proverbial missionary barrel, but I could not part with an old leather coat that was especially comfortable. I gave hundreds of volumes of books to a theological seminary, but kept a few choice ones I could not part with. I gave away about a dozen Bibles, but refused to part with three of my favorite ones.

There is something about the wisdom of old age that puts things in proper perspective. "Timothy, all I want is my warm coat, my few books, and my Scriptures."

Prayer
Gracious Father, help me as I try to sort out the essential from the nonessential. Keep me from becoming enamored by the accumulation of things that really do not matter. Amen.

WHERE HAVE ALL THE PILGRIMS GONE?

Dear brothers, you are only visitors here....
Your real home is in heaven. 1 Peter 2:11

I have a friend who was born and raised in New England. And except for a few years spent at a midwestern college, he never lived anywhere else. Yet, while he loved New England, he had often spoken about spending his retirement years in Florida. When he retired, he and his wife sold the business, their home and all the furniture, and moved south. After a couple of years they moved back to New England. When his wife was asked why they returned, she replied, "It's the same old story. You can take Charlie out of New England, but you can't take New England out of Charlie!"

God has implanted in the heart of every Christian an instinctive longing for a heavenly home. It is hard to shake this yearning. Nevertheless, like Charlie, even though the warm sunshine of Earth is pleasant, and the view of our hopes, our pleasures, and even life's challenges intrigues us, there is a deeper love for our true Homeland—heaven.

I have often wondered why the early believers had such a longing for heaven. I have concluded there were several reasons. For one thing, they held on to this life with a very thin thread. The prospect of martyrdom was a daily expectation. Paul said, "We die daily." The early Christians were never free from the threat of persecution and death.

Furthermore, most of those believers were materially poor. They didn't have much to hold them. There is an interesting paradox in life, that the poorer the Christian is, the more he longs for heaven. How long has it been since you heard a wealthy Christian pray, "Lord, come soon and take me away from all this!"?

Probably the strongest incentive for those first Christians was their strong belief that Jesus would return in their lifetime. They lived with the exciting expectation of the return of Christ and the establishment of his heavenly kingdom. It is the loss of confidence in Christ's return that has dimmed the desire for heaven, and robbed many Christians of their pilgrim nature.

We need to recover this pilgrim concept, if we hope to have a proper perspective of this earthly sojourn. How did the old chorus go? "This world is not my home, I'm just a-passing through."

Prayer
Dear Lord, I thank you for teaching me the transitory nature of life, so that I will not become too deeply entrenched in it. At the same time, keep me from using this knowledge as an excuse to neglect my responsibilities here, or to diminish my appreciation of this life. Amen.

 # PEOPLE ON THE GO

Heaven can be entered only through the narrow gate! The highway to hell is broad, and its gate is wide enough for all the multitudes who choose its easy way. But the Gateway to Life is small, and the road is narrow, and only a few ever find it.
Matthew 7:13, 14

SINCE retirement, we have discovered the ideal way to travel. There are two basic rules: first, never be in a hurry, and second, turn off the expressway at the nearest exit. Nothing will spoil a trip more than the need to be somewhere at a given time, unless it is the abysmal monotony of an expressway. Avoid both like a poison.

My wife and I try to plan our retirement trips by allowing time to travel the older, two lane roads. They are narrower, but certainly less populated with trucks, trailers, mobile homes, and choking diesel-burning behemoths.

Jesus pictures humanity as everlastingly on the go. The roads of life stretch out before us, and from the time we choose our route until we ultimately reach our destination, we are in motion. Where is everybody going? And what are they hoping to find when they arrive? Jesus said that we are looking for the road that leads to Life. But the sad truth is, the multitudes are on the wrong road. They have succumbed to the lure of the expressway—the wide road.

Highway experts tell us that the greatest hazard of the expressway is its tendency to lull the driver to sleep. We set the cruise control at "55," and then lean back and steer. After a while a kind of hypnosis sets in, we forget to observe the basic rules of driving, and we lose the sense of alertness. Jesus said that the vast majority of people are like those desensitized travelers. They like the broad expressway because there are so few restrictions, lots of room to navigate, and they can really make time. So they rush through life to their own destruction.

The choice of roads is ours to make. The one is wide, smooth, and offers the least resistance. The other one is narrower—it has some twists and turns, frequent rough spots, and a few steep hills to climb, but what a glorious view! Perhaps like us, you are disenchanted with the expressway. Then turn off at the nearest exit and journey with Christ on the road that leads to Life. It will be an unforgettable trip.

Prayer
Heavenly Father, I praise you for helping me find the right road, and for the promise of Life, both here, and at the end of the journey. Let me be a guide to others, to direct them to that road that leads to Life. Amen.

LEARNING FROM SHEEP

Because the Lord is my Shepherd, I have everything that I need. Psalm 23:1

COOL, still waters, lush green pastures, the protecting rod and staff of the shepherd! Such is the lot of a trusting sheep. It is not intimidated by dark valleys, or the presence of wild beasts, for the shepherd is its strong protector and provider.

Those of us who are retired can learn a lot from sheep. It almost seems as though David had us in mind when he wrote those comforting words. For the things that concern us—daily provision for our physical needs, freedom from internal and external fears, and assurance of heaven—form the framework of Psalm 23.

In verse 1 David mentions the Lord's provision for our physical needs. "Because the Lord is my Shepherd, I have everything that I need." We have cool water to drink, green pastures to graze in, and the Shepherd's rod and staff to protect us. What more do we need! Sometimes we become so preoccupied with concern for our daily needs that we forget the promise of Philippians 4:19, "It is he who will supply all your needs."

In verse 4 of Psalm 23 David addresses our second major concern, release from nagging fears. "Because the Lord is my Shepherd . . . I will not be afraid." As we grow older, our fears tend to enlarge. If we are not careful, they can dominate and control us. The Shepherd releases us from those binding fears, so that we can walk through the dark valleys of life with confidence and trust.

In verse 6 the Psalmist speaks with assurance about a third area of concern, our eternal destiny. "I will live with you forever in your home." This is our ultimate expectation, to be forever with the Lord! Jesus promised, "There are many homes up there where my Father lives, and I am going to prepare them for your coming" (John 14:2, 3).

So, in this beautifully expressive Psalm we have God's gracious provision, both for here and hereafter. "Your goodness and unfailing kindness shall be with me all of my life, and afterwards I will live with you forever in your home" (v. 6).

Prayer

Strong Shepherd, quiet the fears of my anxious heart, and help me to trust in you as a sheep trusts its shepherd. Go with me when I walk through the dark valleys, and bring me in peace to your eternal home. Amen.

LEAD ME TO THE ROCK

When my heart is faint and overwhelmed, lead me to the mighty, towering Rock of safety. For you are my refuge, a high tower where my enemies can never reach me. Psalm 61:2, 3

DEEP in the Pennsylvania hills, not far from my boyhood home, was a favorite camping place simply called "the Rock." At least, that was the name by which we kids knew it, for not too many people ever saw it. Many of our Saturday hikes ended at the Rock, where we lit our camp fire, spread our blankets, and camped under its overhanging shelter.

David, the Psalmist, had his favorite rock also, and in times of deep distress, or simply when he wanted to be alone, he resorted to it. This is the theme of Psalm 61: the mighty, towering Rock of safety.

It is appropriate that the Scriptures picture Jesus as our Rock, for the rock signifies strength, stability, safety, and shelter. It is encouraging to know that in a world of uncertainty, insecurity, and instability, there is a "mighty, towering Rock."

Some of our most beautiful old Christian hymns speak of this Rock. There is the unforgettable "Rock of ages, cleft for me, let me hide myself in thee." And how often have Christians been strengthened by singing, "On Christ the solid Rock I stand, all other ground is sinking sand." Then there is, "The Lord's our Rock, In Him we hide, A shelter in the time of storm." And many of us have been blessed by singing, "O safe to the Rock that is higher than I. . . ."

Cynics accuse us of a cowardly form of escapism, and ridicule "hiding in Christ" as the "fetal syndrome," a desire to escape back into the security of the womb. But even the self-reliant man or woman of the world has his own form of escapism. For some it is the illusory world of drugs, a personal psychoanalyst, or the false security of money. For my part I would rather take my refuge in the one David calls "the mighty, towering Rock of safety."

It is wisdom, and not cowardice that makes us flee to the shelter of the Rock when the tornado strikes. Only a fool stands out in the storm.

Prayer

Strong Son of God, my Rock and my Fortress, I accept your offer of rest and security in your shadow. In this world of shifting sands, I am grateful to be able to stand upon the solid Rock. Amen.

 # COMMENDABLE FAITH

What is faith? It is the confident assurance that something we want is going to happen . . . even though we cannot see it up ahead. Hebrews 11:1

THIS definition of faith sounds contradictory. How can we be sure of what we can't see? But the old saying, "Seeing is believing," has nothing to do with faith. Faith is believing without seeing.

Thomas had a problem with this. He had said, "I'll believe Jesus was resurrected when I see the evidence—the wounds in his hands." When Jesus appeared to him, and showed him the evidence, he believed. But it is significant that Jesus did not commend him for having faith. There was no need for faith when the proof was obvious.

I want to talk about faith in two dimensions. First, faith as it relates to what we believe about God and his written Word. As Christians, we profess to believe in the inspired, authoritative Word of God. But there are many deep things in the Bible that we cannot comprehend with our finite minds, and it is at this point that our faith becomes active. We reach out with faith believing God has revealed his supernatural truth to us.

Ours is a revealed faith. That is, we could not have

arrived at these truths apart from divine revelation. Paul said that the gospel he preached was not his own, but had been revealed to him by God (Gal. 1:12).

Furthermore, ours is a supernatural faith. It is a faith that transcends our world of natural law. The virgin birth, the miracles of Jesus, and the Resurrection, must be accepted by faith. Therefore, unless we are prepared to believe that what the Bible teaches is both revealed and supernatural, we will never have a biblical faith.

And second, faith is more than something to be believed, it is a life to be lived. It is to be lived out in our conduct, attitudes, and lifestyle. This is what Paul meant in 2 Corinthians 5:7, "We *live* by faith, not by sight" (NIV). This is the practical aspect of our faith.

Do we trust God for our daily needs? Do we believe that he will give us the guidance we need? Do we have faith in the loving providence of God? Do we continue to have faith in the goodness of God, even when everything seems to contradict it? Do we believe that God will watch over us in our declining years, as he has promised? If we do, this is what it means to "live by faith."

Prayer
Forgive me, Father, for my lack of faith. I confess, even as that distraught father once confessed, "Lord, I do believe, but help thou my unbelief." Amen.

DELIGHTING IN GOD'S WILL

I delight to do your will, my God, for your law is written upon my heart! Psalm 40:8

IT is a common mistake to think that God's will is of interest only to the young. We usually think of it in terms of finding a mate, deciding on a life's vocation, or selecting a college to attend. While these are extremely important decisions involving God's will, they are not the only ones we will face in life.

The decision-making process doesn't end when we get married or decide on a career. As we grow older, we find ourselves constantly facing situations that require important decisions—choices. In looking ahead to retirement we must deal with questions involving relocation, changing family relationships, investments, insurance, church selection, and a host of other important matters that require thoughtful decisions.

At this stage of life, the mature Christian no longer needs to ask the question, "Does God have a will for my life?" By this time he knows without a doubt that God does have a plan and purpose for each one of us.

Nature itself teaches us that God never does anything aimlessly. All that he brings into being has purpose. In the Genesis account of creation we are told that after the sixth day of creative activity, "God looked over all that he had made, and it was excellent in every way" (Gen. 1:31).

Not only does nature teach us about God's plan and purpose for his created beings, but our own experience assures us of his will. As we look back over the years of our pilgrimage, we can clearly see the will of God, quietly but powerfully at work.

The knowledge that God the Holy Spirit is in control gives us a sense of assurance and peace about the future. As God has led in the past, so will he continue to lead in the days that lie ahead. And, as a result, we can say with David, "I delight to do your will, my God."

Prayer

Gracious Lord, how grateful I am that you have designed nothing but the best for me. As I look back, I see your steadying hand, guiding and supporting me. And as I look to the future, I go with confidence, knowing that your will is "good, acceptable and perfect." Amen.

HOW MUCH ARE YOU WORTH?

How does a man benefit if he gains the whole world and loses his soul in the process? For is anything worth more than his soul? Mark 8:36, 37

HOW do you measure the value of things? A vase is valuable if it is made of quality material. If the artist is famous, the vase has even more value. And if it is irreplaceable, it can have astronomical value. The same is true of paintings, historical documents, stamps, and figurines.

But God deals in people, and he tells us that the value of each individual surpasses all the so-called "priceless" artifacts. In fact, Jesus said that there is nothing in the entire world that is worth more than you and I. This is a concept that needs to be emphasized in our highly impersonal world, where "things" are often more important than people. And it is especially appropriate for older people, who often tend to think that they are no longer of value to society.

Jesus illustrated the value God places on each person by three similar parables. He told about a lost sheep, a lost coin, and a lost son. Each of these had such value that no effort was spared to find them. The shepherd searched the hills and valleys for the one lost sheep, the housewife turned the house upside down looking for the lost coin, and the father waited anxiously and longingly for the return of his lost son.

These three parables deal with the subject of concern for the lost, and the value of each person. They teach us that God considered us so precious that he allowed his own Son to lay down his life to redeem us. "For God loved the world so much that he gave his only Son so that anyone who believes in him shall not perish but have eternal life" (John 3:16).

Then, too, that we are of worth to God is proved by the fact that he has adopted us into his own family. "To all who received him [Jesus], he gave the right to become children of God" (John 1:12). Think of the value we place upon our own children. There is nothing we would not sacrifice for them. And if our children are of such worth to us, of how much more worth are God's children to him?

If you have been suffering from the worthless feeling syndrome, take heart. Is there anything in all the world that has more value than you? Absolutely not!

Prayer

Heavenly Father, thank you for thinking so highly of me that you sent your own Son to the cross to die for my sins, and to make me whole. And thank you for including me as a member of your family. Amen.

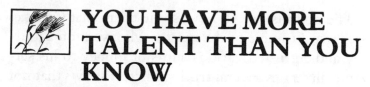

YOU HAVE MORE TALENT THAN YOU KNOW

His master praised him for good work. "You have been faithful in handling this small amount," he told him, "so now I will give you many more responsibilities." Matthew 25:21

ONE day a woman came to see me about her husband. "Since he has retired," she said, "he is impossible to live with. He doesn't seem to know what to do with himself." I asked her what he enjoyed doing most before he retired. She told me that he had been a member of the auxiliary police force in our city, and had loved it. Now, however, they had no further need of him.

I invited the man out to lunch, and told him about a problem we faced at the church, and asked if he could help us. We had changed from one to two morning services, and the traffic around the church on Sunday mornings was a mess. I asked the man how he would like to wear his uniform and bring some order out of the chaos. He was delighted and so was the local police department, for it relieved them of a growing problem as well. The retired policeman formed his own traffic crew from other men in the church, and made a tremendous contribution to the smooth functioning of our Sunday services. And he enjoyed it.

The point is, we all have some talent that God can use. Jesus' parable of the master who went on a journey and entrusted various sums of money to his servants illustrates several truths. First, it shows that not everyone receives the same amount of talents. A talent of silver in the first century was worth about a thousand dollars. In time, the talent came to be thought of as an ability. Like the unwise man in the parable we are tempted to think that because we are less talented than others, we will not invest our abilities.

The whole point of the parable is not how many abilities the Master has given us, but how well are we using what we have? And the theme of accountability comes through loud and clear. Each servant was required to show what he did with his talents when the Master returned.

We may think that we have no abilities that God can use, but no one is totally devoid of talent. Retirement offers us a tremendous opportunity to explore our possibilities for service, and to make an investment of whatever ability God has given to us, great or small. Those who put their talents to work will hear the Master say, "Good work, you are a good and faithful servant."

Prayer
Lord Jesus, forgive me for thinking that my meager abilities are not good enough. I pray that you will lead me as I begin to explore the opportunities for service. Amen.

MY TIME IS GOD'S TIME

Teach us to number our days and recognize how few they are; help us to spend them as we should.
Psalm 90:12

"MY time is your time, your time is my time," Rudy Vallee, a famous crooner of a bygone era, used to sing. The Bible has improved upon that sentiment by stating that our time is God's time.

David confessed to the Lord, "O Lord. . . . You are my God; my times are in your hands" (Ps. 31:14, 15). The word "times" referred to a span of time of unspecified duration. So what David actually said was, "However long may be my sojourn on this earth, my hours, days, weeks, months or years, all belong to God and are under his sovereign control."

Now that we have retired, there is a strong temptation to forget that basic truth. We tend to think that since we no longer need to account for our time to an employer, our time is our own. However, retirement does not mean that God ceases to have any claim upon our time. The happiest retired Christians I have met are those who continue to give the Lord priority over their time.

This is not to say that we must feel guilty about playing golf, traveling, fishing, or other recreational activities. After all, we have earned the right to indulge more frequently in those leisure activities. I have never believed the false philosophy: "It is better to burn out than rust out." You wouldn't say that about your car. My five-year-old car is rusting out, but I'd rather have it than one that burned out the first six months.

On the other hand, there is a danger that we might become so self-indulgent with our time that we fail to properly use our gifts and talents for the Lord's service. There are churches and worthwhile civic organizations that are crying for help and could use the expertise and wisdom of our accumulated experiences. Let us begin to investigate the possibilities that are available. In doing so, we will be saying, "My time is God's time."

Prayer

Dear Lord, forgive me for growing careless about the use of my time. Give me the wisdom to know where I can best invest my time for your greater glory. Amen.

 # HANGING HARPS ON THE WILLOW TREES

Weeping, we sat beside the rivers of Babylon thinking of Jerusalem. We have put away our lyres [harps], hanging them upon the branches of the willow trees, for how can we sing?
Psalm 137:1-3

SINCE retiring and moving to Florida I have met scores of people who, like the Israelites, have found themselves in a strange land, and they are very unhappy. They are here bodily, but their hearts are back in Jerusalem, their true homeland.

Psalm 137 was written during a difficult time in Israel's history. God's people had been carried off by their enemies to languish in exile in distant Babylon. But they were unable to overcome their love for their former homeland, and this became such an obsession that it even interfered with their worship of God. As they gathered by a river in the distant land, they tried to sing their songs of praise to God, but the memory of Jerusalem choked their songs with tears. So, in frustration they hung their harps on the branches of the willow trees and wept, crying, "How can we sing the Lord's song in a strange land?"

Moving to a distant place, leaving old familiar landmarks, friends and family, can indeed be a traumatic experience. But even more tragic, for some people it can interfere with their worship of the Lord. Recently

I talked with a retired couple, and asked them if they had found a church yet, knowing that back home in Michigan they had both been very active. They replied, "No, we have given up trying to find the right church, and don't attend at all anymore."

"Thinking of Jerusalem" can be damaging to our peace of mind. It is far better to accept the events of our lives as further opportunities to serve the Lord. The inability to forget the past, and take advantage of our present, can immobilize us.

Happily, it doesn't need to be that way. My wife and I have found a church where we can contribute our service, we have made a score of new friends to add to the ones we have already, and we have found the beauty of this part of our country to be beyond our expectations.

Perhaps it is time to take the harps off the willow branches, and strike up a song again.

Prayer

Loving Lord, forgive me for failing to see that I can be happy anywhere, as long as you are with me. Thank you for the many wonderful memories of the past, and for the blessings that you have in store for me now. Amen.

WHEN GOD IS NEAR

Seek the Lord while you can find him. Call upon him now while he is near. Isaiah 55:6

THE admonition to call upon the Lord while he is near would seem to indicate that there are times when the Lord is nearer to us than at others. For one thing, most Christians have found the Lord to be near when they have been close to nature. There is something about getting away from the rat race of the city and heading for the hills that increases our awareness of God's nearness.

I remember a particular time in my life when the presence of God was overwhelming. I had been camping out on a mountaintop in the Adirondacks with a sleeping bag and no tent. As I lay there looking out into space and seeing the thousands of stars, I was suddenly overcome with the magnitude of the universe. I sensed the greatness of God, as compared with my own smallness. It was almost as though I could have reached out and touched the Lord, for as David said, "The heavens are telling the glory of God" (Ps. 19:1).

It is also true that God is near when we are going through times of grief and sorrow. God said, "When you go through deep waters and great trouble, I will be with you" (Is. 43:2). When life is going smoothly, and there are no problems, sicknesses, or sorrows, for some reason we do not seem to be as aware of the Lord's presence. But he is there in sunshine and shadow, for he has said, "I will never leave you." Having been a pastor for more than forty years, I have seen Christians go through happy times and sad times. But it is almost always in the sad times that they become more acutely aware of the Lord's nearness.

Then, too, the Lord is near when we gather for worship. Jesus said, "For where two or three gather together . . . I will be right there among them" (Matt. 18:20). There is something awe-inspiring about walking into a quiet sanctuary and joining in worship with other believers. The beauty of the sanctuary can be helpful in creating this spirit, but I have sensed God's presence in a small, cold army chapel, with no stained glass windows, no ornate decorations, and no pipe organ. It seems to me that God is very near whenever we come together with other Christians to worship him in spirit and in truth. That is why the Hebrew writer urged, "Let us not neglect our church meetings, as some people do" (Heb. 10:25). God delights to draw near to those who gather to worship him.

Prayer
Heavenly Father, your Word has promised, "draw close to me, and I will draw close to you." I know that you are ever with me, even though I may not be aware of it. Thank you for your nearness, and the comfort this promise brings to me. Amen.

LONG SERMONS
AND SLEEPY PEOPLE

As Paul spoke on and on, a young man named
Eutychus, sitting on the window sill, went fast
asleep and fell three stories to his death below.
Acts 20:9

WE can all empathize with young Eutychus, for
everyone, at one time or another, has dozed off in
church. When I was a young preacher I used to take
it as a personal affront if anyone fell asleep during my
sermon. Then one Sunday afternoon I happened to
be listening to a recorded replay of my morning message, and I also fell asleep in the middle of it.

In defense of preachers, however, boredom is not
the only reason for drifting off in church. Age, physical condition, medication, and lack of sleep the night
before can all contribute to somnolence.

The upper room had been so crowded when young
Eutychus came in that he had to find a seat in the
open window. Many lamps were burning, and the
room was hot, jammed, and stuffy. We don't know
what time Paul started to preach, but he went on till
midnight. Who could blame the youngster for dozing
off!

Since retiring from the pastoral ministry, I have had
opportunity to become an objective listener to ser-
mons. I have concluded that most of them are too

long. From my new vantage point in the pew, I can look around and tell when the audience has reached its limit of attention. Unfortunately, when I am in the pulpit I tend to be lengthy. As a pastor friend of mine said, "As we preachers get older, everything we say reminds us of something else."

However, in spite of that weakness, I am more convinced than ever that God uses the preaching of his Word to great advantage. The Holy Spirit has a way of filtering out the superfluous verbiage and the nonessential anecdotes. And if we are sensitive to the Spirit's voice, we will always receive something of value from the message. Therefore, we need to expose ourselves to the ministry of God's Word as often as possible. Retirement is no excuse for neglecting this vital area of our lives.

Unfortunately, there is no verse of Scripture that defines the exact length of a sermon. But I think my homiletics professor in seminary hit it right on the head when he said, "In order for a sermon to be immortal, it need not be eternal."

Prayer

Heavenly Father, I thank you for giving shepherds to the church to feed us and nurture us in the faith. Let me be an encouragement to my pastor, and pray for him as he opens up the Word of Life to us. Amen.

THIS LITTLE LIGHT OF MINE

Don't hide your light! Let it shine for all; let your good deeds glow for all to see. Matthew 5:15

ONE evening, a number of years before World War I, a traveler in Europe found himself in the outskirts of a small village nestled in a valley between Saxony and Bohemia. As he approached the town, he heard the ringing of a church bell and saw people making their way to an old church, located on the hill overlooking the town square. He noticed that they were carrying something in their hands, but in the dim light of dusk he could not determine what it was.

Soon the darkened windows of the church began to glow, softly at first, and then with increasingly brighter light. The traveler listened to the sounds of the organ and the singing of ancient hymns, and then the light from the windows faded, as the people filed out. It was then he noticed that each person carried a small oil lamp.

The traveler walked to the town inn where he obtained lodging for the night and asked the proprietor, "Why do all those people carry lamps to evening vespers?" The innkeeper explained that the church was known throughout Europe as "The Church of the

Lighted Lamps." In A.D. 1550, a local baron had built the church for the villagers and had presented it to the townspeople, but with one stipulation. He requested each person to bring his own lamp, for the church had no other light. When the first person entered the church, his lamp was lighted by the pastor's lamp, and he in turn lit the lamp of the one following him, until every lamp was aglow. Consequently, each person who failed to attend vespers was missed, because the light in the church was a little dimmer.

The Christian anywhere who isolates himself from his church and community is depriving them of a stronger light. The absence of his light diminishes his witness. Therefore Jesus says, "Don't hide your light! Let it shine for all." Then in case we don't quite understand what he meant by our "light," he adds, "let your good deeds glow for all to see." Our consistent Christian life becomes our light. As the children often sing, "Don't let Satan snuff it out; I'm gonna let it shine!"

Prayer
Dear Lord, I am only one person, and my light is weak. But I want to be a witness to my family and neighbors of the love of Jesus. Help me to so live that others will see the true Light. Amen.

Musings . . .

Grow old along with me!
The best is yet to be,
The last of life, for which
* the first was made.*
Our times are in his hands.
Robert Browning

I have only just a minute
Only sixty seconds in it.
Forced upon me—can't refuse it.
But it's up to me to use it.
I must suffer if I lose it.
Just a tiny little minute,
But eternity is in it.
Anonymous

I have held many things in my hands and I have
lost them all; but whatever I have placed in God's
hands, that I still possess. Martin Luther

If a man cannot be a Christian where he is, he
cannot be a Christian anywhere.
Henry Ward Beecher

A never-ending source of wonder to me is the way
God continues to reveal new truth to His children,
especially to those who reach an age when they
think they know a few things about the Christian
faith.

As the years went on, I thought, "Surely now in my latter years, I'll be able to put to good use what wisdom I have accumulated." Instead, I have been going through one of the most intense learning periods of my life. Especially in connection with our children and grandchildren. Catherine Marshall

We are not here to be overcome, but to rise unvanquished after every knock-out blow, and laugh the laugh of faith, not fear. Amy Carmichael

Time is a dressmaker specializing in alterations. Faith Baldwin

The future has a habit of suddenly and dramatically becoming the present. Roger W. Babson

God doesn't always give us the wisdom to solve our problems. Sometimes He just lets us know that Jesus can solve them. Malcolm Cronk

Is your place a small place?
Tend it with care!—
He set you there.

Is your place a large place?
Guard it with care!—
He set you there.

What'er your place, it is
Not yours alone, but His
Who set you there.
John Oxenham.

RELATIONSHIPS

YOU SHOULD BE LIKE ONE BIG HAPPY FAMILY, FULL OF SYMPATHY TOWARD EACH OTHER, LOVING ONE ANOTHER WITH TENDER HEARTS AND HUMBLE MINDS . . . . FOR WE ARE TO BE KIND TO OTHERS AND GOD WILL BLESS US FOR IT. 1 Peter 3:8, 9

WALKING WITH GOD

Enoch was sixty-five years old when his son Methuselah was born. . . . then, when he was 365, and in constant touch with God, he disappeared, for God took him! Genesis 5:21-24

SOMEONE has described the fifth chapter of Genesis as "a monotonous chronicle of nobodies." Their names appear for a moment in the early dawn of history, and then they fade away. Nothing is mentioned about their aspirations, dreams, struggles, or hopes. The only thing said of them is that they were born, fathered children, and died.

There is one notable exception, however, and this man's name was Enoch. While all the others were said to have died, Enoch was taken home to God without dying. Furthermore, Enoch was described as a person who was "in constant touch with God."

The Hebrew word *halak,* which is translated "walk," can be used in a variety of ways. It can mean to walk literally, or as translated in *The Living Bible,* to walk figuratively. Enoch lived in such close fellowship with God that he figuratively "walked" with him.

A little girl came home from Sunday school and related to her grandmother the story she had heard about Enoch. "God used to go on long walks with

Enoch, and they talked and talked about many things," explained the child. "One day they had gone on a long, long walk, and Enoch was many miles from his home. So God said to him, 'Enoch, we are a long ways from your house, and it is far past supper time, why don't you come home with me tonight?' So God took Enoch to his home, and he liked it so much that he stayed forever!" What a beautiful picture of Enoch's fellowship with God.

In a small town cemetery in Massachusetts, next to my father's grave, is a stone marking the resting place of a man who died in 1910. Underneath the name and dates is this simple, four word epitaph, "He walked with God." What a wonderful tribute by his family. Such a life is possible for each of us, but like Enoch, we must "be in constant touch with God."

Prayer

O Master, let me walk with thee
In lowly paths of service free;
Tell me thy secret, help me bear
The strain of toil, the fret of care. Amen.

BEARING CHRIST'S BRAND MARK

I carry on my body the scars of the whippings and wounds from Jesus' enemies that mark me as his slave. Galatians 6:17

IT was common in the first century to brand slaves with the mark of the owners. Lloyd Douglas brings this out so graphically in his book *The Robe*. He describes Demetrius, the slave, who was branded in his ear lobe. Others received indelible marks on their face or foreheads. Even though a slave was eventually set free, he could not erase the former owner's brand mark.

Paul takes this experience and applies it to his own relationship to Christ. He says that the scars he received from his many beatings for the cause of his Savior identified him as Christ's bond slave.

While it is true that there have been hundreds of thousands of believers who have literally suffered physical abuse, and even death, because of their Christian faith, the vast majority of us have never had to bear any such marks. We should be eternally grateful to God that in the Free World we can express our faith in Christ without suffering physical abuse. At the same time, we must be in prayer for those thousands of fellow believers behind the Iron Curtain, who

83

are enduring incredible physical and mental persecution for Christ's sake.

But there are other identifying marks that brand us as belonging to Christ. We are marked by our love for others. Jesus said, "Your strong love for each other will prove to the world that you are my disciples" (John 13:35). We are also marked by a sincere concern for the needs of those around us. That means for those who are lonely, the poor, the grieving, and the sick. Furthermore, we will be marked by a morally upright life. Our religious profession will be consistent with our lifestyle. These are a few of the identifying marks that brand us as belonging to Christ.

Recently I was at a gathering of people who were all strangers to me. One of them was a lovely woman in her eighties. She had such a kind, radiant smile and such a gracious manner that I thought she must surely be a Christian. After chatting with her a short while, I said, "You must be a Christian." "Oh yes," she replied, "I have known the Lord for many years, but how did you know?" I replied, "You bear the brand marks of Christ."

Prayer
Lord Jesus, I want my life to bear witness to the fact that I belong to you. Give me the grace and strength to so live that others will recognize that you are my Lord and Savior, and will want to know you also. Amen.

 # GOD KNOWS YOUR NAME

The Lord who created you . . . says, "Don't be afraid, for I have ransomed you; I have called you by name; you are mine." Isaiah 43:1

The sheep hear his voice and come to him; and he calls his own sheep by name and leads them out. John 10:3

IT was Christmastime, and the store was crowded. A small lost girl began to cry. People tried to comfort her, but she only became more frantic. Then a man's voice was heard above the din of the crowd, calling, "Jeannie! Jeannie!" Immediately the child stopped crying as she recognized her father's voice, and in a moment she was swept up in his arms. What all the other well-meaning shoppers could not do for her was accomplished by the voice of one who knew her name.

If you have had occasion to call the Social Security office, you have discovered that the first question is not "What is your name?" Rather, the receptionist asks, "What is your Social Security number?" Being identified by a number is impersonal, and leaves you feeling empty, unimportant. The real you feels lost.

In our world of four billion people, it is a staggering thought that the Lord Jesus Christ knows each of us by name. The Lord God said to his people, "Don't be afraid . . . I have called you by name; you are mine." It is comforting and reassuring to be called by name. Jesus, the Good Shepherd, reaffirmed that promise of the Old Covenant when he said, "I know my sheep and call them by name."

As David wrote in Psalm 139: "O Lord, you have examined my heart and know everything about me. . . . This is too glorious, too wonderful to believe! I can never be lost to your Spirit! . . . You saw me before I was born and scheduled each day of my life before I began to breathe. . . . How precious it is, Lord, to realize that you are thinking about me constantly . . ." (vv. 1–18).

Prayer

I am comforted by the words of the Psalmist who reminds me "Every moment you know where I am." Thank you for knowing me, knowing me by name, making me part of your family, and "leading me along the path of everlasting life." Amen.

WE BELONG TO GOD'S FAMILY

To all who received him, he gave the right to become the children of God. John 1:12

SEVERAL years ago I had gone with a group of college students to conduct a worship service in the chapel of a convalescent home. Following the service we visited in the rooms of those who were unable to attend the chapel service. A man who said he was ninety-three grasped me by the hand as I was leaving and said sadly, "My entire family has gone, and I am the only one left." Since he had told me that he was a Christian, I responded, "That is not entirely true, for you still have the whole family of God."

It is a comforting thought that even though our parents have died, and perhaps even all other members of our family, we are surrounded by our heavenly Father, and a large family of brothers and sisters in Christ. There is a wonderfully encouraging statement concerning this in Romans 8:16, "His Holy Spirit speaks to us deep in our hearts, and tells us that we really are God's children."

Bishop Moule once related how from time to time he had been tempted to doubt that he really belonged to God. He wrote, "When I am tempted to doubt, the Holy Spirit comes to me and says, 'Without doubt you *are* his child.' And my wondering, believing spirit replies, 'Without doubt he *is* my Father.'"

A Christian couple told me about an interesting conversation that occurred at their dinner table one evening. Their six-year-old boy spoke up and startled the parents by asking, "Do I really belong to you?" They had no idea what prompted the question, but they reassured him that he was truly their son. Several days later it came out that on a television newscast he had heard about a mix-up at a hospital where a mother had been given the wrong child. The youngster wanted reassurance that he really belonged to his father and mother.

What an encouragement to know, that as a result of receiving Jesus as our Lord and Savior, we receive the "right to become [the] children of God." As Paul said, "His Holy Spirit speaks to us deep in our hearts, and tells us that we really are God's children." We belong to God's family!

Prayer
Heavenly Father, I praise you for the great privilege of calling you my Father. And I praise you also for surrounding me with many brothers and sisters who encourage me and provide family of God fellowship. Help me to love each of them as you do, and to be sensitive to their needs. Amen.

HAVE YOU SAID "I LOVE YOU" LATELY?

After breakfast Jesus said to Simon Peter, "Simon, son of John, do you love me more than these others?" John 21:15

AN older couple was sitting in a restaurant, enjoying a good meal, when they overheard a conversation at the next table. The young man had reached across the table and taken his young bride's hands in his. He said, "Darling, I love you." Whereupon the older lady said to her husband, "Dear, it has been a long time since you told me that you love me." He replied, somewhat gruffly, "I told you once that I love you, and if I change my mind, I'll let you know."

It is only a story, of course, but the point is well taken. Love needs to be expressed verbally as well as actively. Husbands and wives need to hear it. So do parents and children. And so does the Lord. Peter was somewhat reluctant to express his love to Jesus verbally, so he hedged. Jesus tried three times to get him to say, "I love you," but Peter never quite rose to the occasion. It is significant that Jesus did not ask, "Peter, have you served me?" Love must precede service if the service is to be effective.

This principle was expressed so touchingly in the musical play, *Fiddler on the Roof.* In that marvelous scene, Tevye kept trying to get his wife Golda to admit that she loved him. Each time he asked, "Do you love me?" she replied by reminding him that she had been a dutiful wife, darning his socks, milking his cows, cooking his meals, and giving him children. But Tevye, who is longing to hear her express her love verbally, persists, "But do you love me?" Shyly she responds, "I suppose I do." Then Tevye replies, "And I suppose I love you too." And in the concluding chorus, he sings triumphantly, "It doesn't change a thing, but even so, after twenty-five years, it's nice to know."

Prayer
Dear Lord, I do love you. Forgive me for failing to express it as often as I should, and for taking your love for me for granted. I pray that I will be more careful to express my love to those around me. Amen.

 # LOVE IS FOR KEEPS

There are three things that remain—faith, hope, and love—and the greatest of these is love.
1 Corinthians 13:13

IT was a beautiful day in Chicago, and the people lying on the beach were in a holiday mood. Soon every head was turned toward the sky as a small airplane was seen belching out a trail of white smoke. At first they thought the pilot was in trouble, but then they noticed that the smoke was beginning to form letters in the sky. As the plane dipped and climbed, the message "I love you" became discernible. By this time a traffic jam had occurred in the Loop as hundreds of shoppers stopped to read the words emblazoned boldly on the clear sky.

The switchboards were soon jammed as scores of curious people called to inquire about the mysterious message. Who was the unknown pilot, and what had prompted him to write such a message, and for whom was it intended? Finally, after the story had faded from everybody's memory, the culprit confessed. A seventy-two-year-old man, formerly a stunt pilot, had written the message to his wife in celebration of their fiftieth wedding anniversary. After fifty years, their love was just as bright and alive as the day they were married.

One thing we can say about real love is that it is for keeps. That is the primary note in Paul's masterful description of love in 1 Corinthians 13. In verse 8 he says, "All the special gifts and powers from God will someday come to an end, but love goes on forever." And in his conclusion he reminds us that of the few things that will endure in life, "the greatest . . . is love."

When I served as a campus chaplain, the most frequent question asked of me by college students was, "How do you know when you really love someone?" My answer was, "Read 1 Corinthians 13:4-7, and use it as a checklist." There are ten tests of love found in these few verses. Is the love I profess patient, kind, never envious, not proud, courteous, unselfish, good-natured, non-vindictive, sympathetic, and dependable? (If you score 100 percent on this test, you should be canonized and sent on ahead.) Unselfish, accepting love, which is a reflection of God's love, will endure.

Prayer
Father, as I examine Paul's description of love, I confess that I fall far short of your expectations. I pray that you will point out to me those areas where my love is weakest, and strengthen me that I may truly reflect your love to all. Amen.

BREAKING UP THE NEST

He spreads his wings over them,
Even as an eagle overspreads her young.
She carries them upon her wings—
As does the Lord his people!
Deuteronomy 32:11

IN comparing notes with another retired man recently, we discovered that our children are the same ages. He said laughingly, "We thought the day would never come, but ten years ago we kicked the last one out of the nest, and then headed for Florida!"

My wife and I remember the day our youngest son walked the aisle with his bride. We were proud and happy for him, but the moment was tinged with sadness. We returned home that evening and sat down to dinner. Now there were only two of us where once there had been five.

But this is the way of life. Even nature teaches us that there is a time for breaking up the nest. A number of translators and Bible commentators use the older phrase in verse 11 "as an eagle *stirs up* her nest . . . so the Lord." Ornithologists tell us that stirring up the nest is precisely what a parent eagle does. When she feels it is time for the young eaglets to fly, she will actually break up the nest, sometimes pushing it off a cliff. If any of the young birds fail to fly, she will swoop under them, carrying them upon her wings.

This is a beautiful analogy. Moses says this is how the Lord deals with his children. Like that mother eagle, our strong Savior spreads his wings over us. He nourishes us until we are mature in the faith, and then he pushes us out of the nest and we begin to fly on our own. However, should we ever begin to fall, he will pick us up and carry us on his wings.

Many Christians find it hard to leave the nest; it is so warm and cozy, and there is always adequate food. It is much more comfortable to sit in a Bible study several times a week than to visit a sick person, or to teach a Sunday school class, or to witness to neighbors. But this is all a part of "growing up" in the Lord. Perhaps it is time to break up the nest.

Prayer
Heavenly Father, forgive me if I have resisted your efforts to leave the warm nest. Help me to begin to serve, rather than being served. I want to take my place as a strong, mature Christian, and to help those who are in need. Amen.

THE BOOK OF LIFE

Everyone who conquers will be clothed in white, and I will not erase his name from the Book of Life. Revelation 3:5

YOU who are of the same vintage as I will remember the old family Bible. It occupied a prominent place in the parlor, and there was scarcely a home anywhere without one. There were pages in the front of the family Bible for listing the family genealogy—for a record of marriages, births, and deaths.

Unfortunately, as people have ceased to read the Bible, the custom has almost become extinct. Its demise was illustrated by the little boy, who after hearing the pastor refer to "that grand old Book we all read and love," whispered to his mother, "Is he talking about the Sears Roebuck catalog?"

The idea of God's record of humanity being kept in a book is derived from the ancient custom of keeping genealogical records. From early times communities kept their records of citizens. Nehemiah tells about finding such a record in Jerusalem when he returned from exile in Babylon. David prayed that his enemies might "be blotted from the list of the living" (Ps. 69:28).

As far back as Moses, the Lord said, "Whoever has

sinned against me will be blotted out of my book" (Ex. 32:33). And in Philippians 4:3 Paul refers to "my fellow workers whose names are written in the Book of Life." And the last book in the Bible mentions this "Book of Life" seven times.

From an examination of these references, it would appear that the name of each person born into the world is recorded. Not that God has a huge ledger book; but every individual is known by God. It would also appear that those individuals who reject the Lord and refuse to follow him will be "blotted out of the Book of Life." On the other hand, those who submit themselves to the Lord in faith, and trust him as their Savior, will never be erased from the Book of Life. As our text promises, "I will not erase his name from the Book of Life." It is appropriate for each of us to ask, with the words of the old hymn, "Is *my* name written there, on that page bright and fair?"

Prayer

Dear Father, I thank you that you are concerned about every human being. And that even the sparrows are known to you. I am grateful that you have recorded my name among those who are your followers. Help me to be more faithful in sharing this with others. Amen.

RESENTMENT CAN DESTROY YOU

But it is right to celebrate. For he is your brother; and he was dead and has come back to life! He was lost and is found! Luke 15:32

MANY who read the parable of the prodigal son miss the central message of the story. In order to appreciate all of what happens, it is necessary to look at the event that precipitated the story. A group of rather low-down sinners had come to Jesus. This caused deep resentment among some religious people. So Jesus told them all a story about two brothers, one who was very sinful, and the other who was very righteous. In the story, when the sinful brother wised up, he came home to his father's house. The father knocked himself out to show how glad he was to see the sinner repent and return.

Enter now the true villain, the central character in the story. This is the prodigal's brother. When he learned that his brother had returned, and saw the big party his dad had thrown to celebrate the occasion, the older brother "became angry and would not go in." Even though his father came out and begged him to join the festivities, he stubbornly refused, and expressed his bitter resentment by saying, "I've been a model son all these years, I've never crossed you, or stepped out of line, and I have been a hard worker. Yet you never threw a party for me. But when this sinful son of yours comes home, nothing is too good for him!"

So his resentment caused him to miss the party. The self-righteous people who had expressed their resentment against Christ for welcoming sinful people would have had to be blind not to recognize themselves as the villains of Jesus' story.

This parable shows us how our resentments can hinder us from getting God's best out of life. Sometimes the hostility that we feel toward others is simply the result of hidden resentments.

I remember battling with this problem a number of years ago. I had accepted a call to a dying church, and labored sacrificially for five years to make it strong. I turned down offers of raises so the church would have more money for programs. After I left that church, a new pastor was called. He had been there only two years when the church gave him and his wife a trip to the Holy Land as an anniversary present. When I heard this, the resentment I felt toward the church and the new pastor almost destroyed me for a time. Months went by before I could honestly rejoice over his good fortune.

A significant lesson of the prodigal son story is the destructive nature of resentment. It can cause us to miss the party.

Prayer
Heavenly Father, enable me to root out of my heart any hidden envy or resentment against others. I want to "rejoice with those who rejoice, and weep with those who weep." Amen.

IT'S GREAT TO HAVE A FRIEND IN HIGH PLACES

"The greatest love is shown when a person lays down his life for his friends; and you are my friends if you obey me. I no longer call you slaves, for a master doesn't confide in his slaves; now you are my friends. . . ." John 15:13-15

BEN Franklin said somewhat cynically at the close of his life, "I have only three faithful friends remaining: an old wife, an old dog, and ready money." What a pathetic confession from one who had known hundreds of people, many of them of international fame.

The poet Joseph Parry writes about the value of nurturing friendships:

Cherish friendships in your breast;
New is good, but old is best.
Make new friends, but keep the old;
Those are silver, these are gold.

As we grow older we do find our circle of friends narrowing. When we were in school, we thought we would never forget our classmates. But time has a way of dimming those relationships. Our friends graduate, move to distant parts of the country, get married and raise families. They become involved in careers, form new circles of friends, and gradually fade from memory. Finally, even the annual Christmas cards cease.

This is indeed tragic. Boswell wrote, "To let friendships die away by negligence or silence is certainly not wise. It is to voluntarily throw away one of the greatest comforts of this weary pilgrimage."

There is one friendship so valuable we never want to let it die.

Jesus referred to those who were obedient to him as "my friends." And he said that the greatest proof of such friendship is willingness to "lay down one's life for his friends." This Jesus himself did, when he voluntarily died to save us. Can we neglect so great a friend?

It was said of Abraham, "He was . . . a friend of God" (Jas. 2:23). The biblical writers might have said of him that he was a great leader, a man of towering faith, and an example to his people. Instead, his epitaph read, "Abraham, a friend of God."

We may count among our friends many notable people. But there is no higher privilege than having the Lord Jesus Christ as our friend.

Prayer

Dear Lord Jesus, you are indeed a "friend who sticks closer than a brother." During my lifetime I have lost a number of good friends, some by death, some by neglect, and some who have just drifted away. I thank you that you will always be my friend, and nothing will ever separate us. Amen.

OUR FAMILY TREE

You have been chosen by God himself—you are priests of the King, you are holy and pure, you are God's very own—all this so that you may show to others how God called you out of the darkness into his wonderful light. Once you were less than nothing; now you are God's own.
1 Peter 2:9, 10

NOT many of us can boast of a notable family tree. In fact, in most cases, the best thing to do with a family tree is to spray it!

Recently some friends and I got into a friendly discussion about family genealogy. One friend boasted of the many doctors, lawyers, and politicians there were in his family tree. Another one claimed to be related to one of our former presidents. Not to be outdone, I very smugly reminded them that I came from a long line of kings and priests, and quoted the above text as proof.

Here Peter is talking about a Christian's family tree, and reminds his readers that they, along with us, belong to God's family. Furthermore, this is no ordinary family, for it is composed of royalty, priests, and people of purity and virtue. This is a family tree to be proud of!

While Peter was writing to Jewish Christians who would understand the references to Judaism, the terms he used are applicable to Christians of all generations.

Twice he says that we were chosen to be "God's very own." We were chosen, not on the basis of our worthiness, but on the basis of our faith in Christ. "To all who received him, he gave the right to become children of God" (John 1:12). And as God's children, we become a part of that family that traces its roots all the way back to the beginning of the human race.

Then, too, this family tree can boast of "royal priests." It was no light honor for a Jewish priest to be appointed to minister to the king and his court. As members of God's family it is also our privilege to serve the King of Kings. We offer up to God our praise and adoration, and the sacrifices of a pure and holy life. In addition to this, as priests of the King, we intercede on behalf of the people. We show to others how God has "called [us] out of darkness into his wonderful light."

Let the people of the world boast that they can trace their family tree back to the Mayflower. The Christian's family tree is rooted in the eternal purposes of God, even before the world began. You can't go back much farther than that!

Prayer
Father, I praise you for including me as a member of your family. It is a privilege to minister to the world as your priest. I pray that you will use my witness to bring many into your light. Amen.

 # COUNSEL FROM A CENTENARIAN

Don't be afraid, for the Lord will go before you and will be with you; he will not fail nor forsake you. Deuteronomy 31:8

MOSES spoke these words of assurance when he was more than one hundred years old. Speaking out of a wealth of experience, Moses was promising his people that the Lord would never leave or forsake them. That promise was reaffirmed thousands of years later by the Hebrew author who wrote, "For God has said, 'I will never, *never* fail you nor forsake you'" (Heb. 13:5).

There is no language to adequately describe the anguish of forsakenness. Years ago *Life* magazine published a full page picture of a forlorn four-year-old girl standing in the huge cavern of Grand Central Station, clutching a rag doll, and wearing a look of pathetic bewilderment. For some unknown reason her mother had abandoned her there. The caption beneath the picture said simply, "Forsaken."

Another heartbreaking scene occurred two thousand years ago. Jesus was hanging upon a cross, bearing the whole weight of the world's sins. In desperate agony he cried, "My God, my God, why have you forsaken me?" Our sins had caused God to turn away from the Son in that last moment, and our Savior suffered the agony of the forsaken.

But there is a bright side to all of this. Because Jesus was willing to endure the anguish of the forsaken, we will never need to endure it. We may suffer alienation from others, but never from the One who promised, "I will never fail you nor forsake you."

Prayer
Lord, at this time of life when we are feeling most abandoned, we reach out to you and gratefully accept your promise never to forsake us. Thank you for this encouragement. Amen.

Musings . . .

Empathy is your pain in my heart.
Halford E. Luccock

Our heart is in heaven, our home is not here.
Reginald Heber
Hymns: Fourth Sunday in Advent

*The promises of God are just as good as ready
money any day.* Billy Bray

The elixir of eternal youth is wonder. *So long
as a man can find new things at which to wonder, he need never grow old. In this world of
God's, and in the world of human relationships,
he need never lack for that.* William Barclay

*Give us open eyes, Our Father, to see the
beauty all around us and to see it in thy handi-
work. Let all lovely things fill us with gladness
and let them lift up our hearts in true worship.*

*Give us this day, O God, a strong and vivid
sense that thou art by our side. By thy grace, let
us go nowhere this day where thou canst not
come, nor court any companionship that would
rob us of thine.* Peter Marshall

*Kindness goes a long way lots of times when it
ought to stay at home.* Frank McKinney
Hubbard

Christians love one another. They never fail to help widows; they save orphans from those who would hurt them. If a man has something, he gives freely to the man who has nothing. If they see a stranger, Christians take him home and are happy, as though he were a real brother. This is really a new kind of person. There is something divine in them. Aristides, a 2nd-century Roman

"I can forgive, but I cannot forget" is only another way of saying, "I will not forgive." Henry Ward Beecher

It is one of the most beautiful compensations of life that no man can sincerely try to help another, without helping himself. J. P. Webster

For his Holy Spirit speaks to us deep in our hearts, and tells us that we really are God's children. Romans 8:16

Now you can have real love for everyone because your souls have been cleansed from selfishness and hatred when you trusted Christ to save you; so see to it that you really do love each other warmly, with all your hearts. 1 Peter 1:22

MEDITATIONS

RENEWAL

THEY THAT WAIT UPON THE LORD SHALL RENEW THEIR STRENGTH. THEY SHALL MOUNT UP WITH WINGS LIKE EAGLES; THEY SHALL RUN AND NOT BE WEARY; THEY SHALL WALK AND NOT FAINT.
Isaiah 40:31

A DAILY DEVOTIONAL TIME ...WHO NEEDS IT?

The next morning he [Jesus] was up long before daybreak and went out alone into the wilderness to pray. Mark 1:35

WHO needs a daily time for devotions? That question has been answered in God's Word. For one, Jesus needed quiet times. Not only did he enjoy his morning prayer break, we are told that he also went out to the hills in the evening to spend time with the Father (Matt. 14:23). There are numerous other occasions mentioned in the Bible where Jesus prayed alone.

If the strong Son of God in his humanity felt the need of frequent times alone with God, it is obvious that we need such times also. David, who is mentioned in Scripture as "a man after God's own heart," came before the Lord morning, noon, and night. In the Psalms he wrote, "I will pray morning, noon, and night, pleading aloud with God; and he will hear and answer" (Ps. 55:17).

No matter how mature we become in the faith, or how experienced in years, we never outgrow our need for constant communication with the Lord. Prayer and quietness with God is one of the means whereby we learn to know the Lord and understand his Word.

As we meditate we are developing spiritual muscles and strengthening our faith.

I make a distinction between a "devotional" time, and a time of Bible study. The terms are self-explanatory. A devotional is a time of expressing our love and devotion to the Lord. This may be done by prayer, singing, reading Scripture that is devotional in nature, or simply quiet meditation on the attributes of God. The reading of the psalms aloud is an excellent way of expressing our devotion to God. I remember a student at the college I served who would go off by himself with an old hymnal and sing to the Lord. He said that he learned more about praising the Lord in this way than in anything else.

On the other hand, a Bible study may or may not be devotional. Sometimes we can become so caught up in a critical analysis of the text that we lose the devotional aspect. Nevertheless, a regular time of Bible study is vital to our spiritual growth. But it should augment, not supplant, our devotional time.

So, brothers and sisters, we are not too old, nor too young, to begin to establish regular times for the expression of our love to the Lord, and for digging deeper into his Word.

Prayer
Loving Father, forgive my neglect of a daily time with you. Help me in my determination to establish a regular time for expressing my love and gratitude. Amen.

 # SOMETHING TO THINK ABOUT

Fix your thoughts on what is true and good and right. Think about things that are pure and lovely, and dwell on the fine, good things in others. Think about all you can praise God for and be glad about. Philippians 4:8

ONE of the nice features about retirement is the availability of time to think. We didn't have much time for that in the past, but now it has become a luxury we can afford. Unfortunately, for many retirees it is the *only* luxury they can afford. How liberating it is to sit for an hour or more, reflecting upon whatever comes to mind, without a qualm of conscience.

But thinking can be dangerous, as well as edifying. To sit and brood over past mistakes and sins can be deadening. Or to let our minds dwell upon thoughts of envy, jealousy, or self-pity can be debilitating. If we are going to enjoy thinking, we must follow some guidelines.

Paul, in Philippians 4:8, gives specific guidelines for gratifying thinking. He instructs us to fix our thoughts upon lofty ideas, to let our minds soar to noble subjects.

These exalted ideas Paul mentions are matters that relate to truth, honesty, justice, purity, loveliness, and praise. These are all positive, desirable things and worthy of our thoughts. But it will require a great deal of discipline if we want to keep our thoughts from straying to the negative. We need to get hold of one thought and chew on it as a cow chews its cud. Let us take one example from our text. Paul advises us to "think about all you can praise God for." Some people may want to write down all the items for praise that come to mind. Be prepared to discover you have a rather long list.

The Bible uses another word to express this idea of thinking. It is the word "meditation," used primarily in the Old Testament. It means "to ponder or reflect." Genesis 24:63 gives a beautiful picture of Isaac, about to meet his bride for the first time, going out into the fields to meditate.

Today is a good day to begin to cultivate the habit of quiet reflection. There is a lot to think about.

Prayer
Dear Father, I have so much for which to praise you, and there is so much in your Word to occupy my thoughts. Give me the desire to meditate upon those things which build up, rather than destroy. Amen.

# GOD WON'T LET YOU DOWN

No one will be able to oppose you as long as you live, for I will be with you just as I was with Moses. I will not abandon you or fail to help you.
Joshua 1:5

GOD'S word to Joshua was sorely needed. The people of Israel had journeyed long and far under Moses, and some of them had begun to ask, "Have you brought us this far, only to die in the wilderness?" And now that Moses had died, they were even more frightened. So the Lord spoke to Joshua and assured the Israelites that he had not abandoned them or forsaken them in their need.

The Hebrew word *azab* which has been translated "forsake" or "abandon" literally means "to loosen or relinquish hold of." It presents a vivid picture of someone dangling over the edge of a precipice, being held in the strong grip of his rescuer.

People who have retired should have no difficulty in identifying with the Israelites at this point in their journey. They have traveled far, over many weary miles and years, and sometimes feel like crying out, "Lord, have you brought us this far, only to abandon us?" And God responds, "No, I will not abandon you, or fail to help you." This is strong encouragement.

It is important to note that God did not promise

Joshua that he would never experience any discouragements or difficult times in his journey. That would have been unrealistic. Rather, he promised that when Joshua would find himself in trouble, God would hold on to him with his almighty grip and not let him fall.

In reading the life stories of the great saints of the Bible, I have noticed how this fear of abandonment became more prevalent as they grew older. David, Abraham, Isaiah, and others experienced their times of apprehension. It was also true of Luther, Wesley, Edwards, and other great leaders of the church. But through it all the strong hand of God held them.

And the same Lord who encouraged Joshua will also hold on to you. "I will not abandon you or fail to help you."

Prayer

Dear Father, at this time of life when I feel most dependent and helpless, I pray for your strong hand to hold me. I thank you for the assurance that you will never let me down. Amen.

 # A CHANGE OF CLOTHING

You must be a new and different person, holy and good. Clothe yourself with this new nature.
Ephesians 4:24

THE fourth chapter of Ephesians deals with the new lifestyle of the Christian. Paul uses an analogy concerning the old and new nature. He suggests that we take off the old nature and don the new, just as we change our soiled clothing for fresh, clean garments.

As a boy, I learned to appreciate this analogy. A young friend and I had decided to emulate David and go hunting for squirrels with slingshots. We soon came face to face with a beautiful, black-and-white striped kitten. At least, we assumed that it was a kitten. We did not realize it was a skunk. Until it was too late!

We beat a hasty retreat and headed home. As we passed through town, we soon discovered that we were the center of attention, and almost enjoying the unaccustomed notoriety. Needless to say, when I arrived home, there was a mild panic.

My mother divested me of my offensive garments, and threw me into a tub of water, along with a bar of strong, brown Octagon soap, which we usually used on Rover. My father gingerly picked up my clothing and carried them to the end of the yard, where he gave them a decent burial. After the bath and fresh, clean clothing, I was socially acceptable again.

I thought of that skunk experience when I read J. B. Phillip's paraphrase of Ephesians 5:22: "Fling off the old dirty clothes of the old way of living, and put on the fresh, clean clothes of the new life." If there is any one thing clearly stated in the Scriptures, it is that becoming a Christian makes a difference in our lifestyle.

Paul's analogy of clothing yourself with a new nature is not a once and for all action. He doesn't say that we change natures once, and that takes care of it for life. Instead, it is an everyday change of attitudes and thoughts "constantly changing for the better" (Eph. 5:23).

Keep in mind that the person who only changes his socks once in a lifetime will soon find himself persona non grata. Let's throw away the clothing of our old natures often and enjoy our new natures—our new lives in Christ.

Prayer
Dear Lord, so often the old nature seems to get the best of me. I earnestly desire to be clean and pure, and to be the kind of person who is attractive to others. With your help I can fling aside the soiled garments, and put on the fresh, clean clothes of my new life. Amen.

PATCHED PANTS AND BROKEN BOTTLES

"Who would patch an old garment with unshrunk cloth. . . . and who would use old wineskins to store new wine?" Matthew 9:16, 17

WE always have to explain the above parables to our younger generation. Those of us who grew up in the pre-sanforized and pre-disposable era need no commentary. We remember how our mothers always bought our shirts and pants at least two sizes too large in order to allow for shrinkage at the first washing. Back then no mother in her right mind would sew a patch of unshrunken cloth over a hole in an old pair of pants. The first rainstorm would prove embarrassing, as the patch would shrink and tear away, exposing us and the hole to the elements.

It is also necessary to explain about the wine bottles. Back in biblical days, wine was stored in bottles made of leather—new wineskins. When the leather became old, it became hard and brittle. Therefore, knowing that fermenting wine expands, no one would think of pouring new, unfermented wine into old wineskins. The old skins would break open; the new skins would stretch and accommodate the expanding wine.

The key words in the above parables are "old" and "new." The issue was raised by the disciples of John the Baptist, who wanted to know why they were required to observe the old ceremonial laws, especially fasting, and Christ's disciples were not. By use of the two parables Jesus taught them that the old, legalistic ceremonies cannot contain the new life in the Spirit. This new life is a powerful force that cannot be restricted to mere rituals. It can't be patched over or bottled up.

The question is, do we want that new life that Jesus called the "more abundant life"? If so, we must open ourselves up to the growing, expansive power of the Holy Spirit. Otherwise, we will have to go back to wearing patched pants, and drinking from broken bottles.

Prayer
Fill my cup, Lord, I lift it up, Lord,
Come and quench this thirsting of my soul;
Bread of heaven, feed me till I want no more,
Fill my cup, fill it up and make me whole! Amen.

 REKINDLE THE WONDER

When we preached to you, you didn't think of the words we spoke as being just our own, but you accepted what we said as the very Word of God— which of course it was—and it changed your lives when you believed it. 1 Thessalonians 2:13

A group of Sunday school children were asked by their teacher to write a letter to God expressing their thoughts about God's Word, the Bible. One child wrote, "You sure have neat stories. Who gave them to you?" Another one wrote, "I liked your Book. When will you write another one?" The letter I appreciated most was written by a boy who responded with enthusiasm, "I sure like your exciting stories. You really put a lot of zip in them."

Sometimes, after decades of reading the same Book, we lose the excitement expressed by those children. The stories are too well known, the doctrines have become brittle with analysis, and the "zip" has gone out of the Word for us. We need to rekindle that sense of wonder expressed by J. B. Phillips when he set out to translate the Scriptures. In his first edition of *Letters to Young Churches,* he wrote that he often felt like an electrician rewiring an ancient house with the current turned on.

It was something like this with the Thessalonian Christians. They sensed that the message Paul preached was not just a new philosophical idea. Rather, they accepted Paul's teaching as "the very Word of God." And the proof of this was in the results it produced. "It changed your lives when you believed it."

The real test of our belief in the Word of God is in its results. Have the truths we read made any difference in our lifestyle? Have they made us better people? Are we morally and spiritually stronger as a result of hearing the Word? Paul wrote, "When someone becomes a Christian he becomes a brand new person inside. He is not the same any more. A new life has begun!" (2 Cor. 5:17).

When Augustine became a Christian after years of sinful indulgence, he was met by one of his past lovers, who called, "Augustine, don't you know me? It is I." Augustine replied, "Yes, but it is no longer I!" That is the crucial difference.

Prayer

Lord Jesus, I pray that you will restore to me the wonder and reverential awe that I once felt for your Word. Make it come alive to my heart, and be a life-changing force in the days to come. Thank you for your Word, which truly is living and powerful. Amen.

TREES BY THE RIVER

They [believers] are like trees along a river bank bearing luscious fruit each season without fail. Their leaves shall never wither, and all they do shall prosper. Psalm 1:3

TAKE a drive with me on the Jericho road as it winds down from the heights of Jerusalem. Leaving the out-skirts of the city of God, we soon find ourselves in barren wasteland. We see acres of sand and rock, but only a few struggling trees and bushes. The land is arid, dry, and wild. A fitting landscape for Jesus' par-able about the man who was attacked by highwaymen while on that same road.

As we approach the plains of Jericho, where the Jordan River flows to the south, we begin to see lush grass, green plants, and tall trees swaying in the wind. It is easy to find the river, for it is lined with all manner of fruit-bearing trees.

David uses such a scene as this to describe the fol-lowers of God. He says "they are like trees along a river bank, bearing luscious fruit." Most translations read, "They are like trees that have been *planted* by the river." In other words, they were not there because a bird or the wind dropped a careless seed by the river, but they were deliberately planted there. Whoever had planted those trees by the river had done so with purpose. He knew that trees flourished best when allowed to grow near the water.

The analogy is quite clear. You and I are not products of blind chance. But like those trees along the Jordan, we were taken by the loving hands of God and placed where we could draw nourishment from the life-giving stream, the one who is the "Water of Life." And because of this, our lives bear fruit for God.

And the good news is, "their leaves shall never wither." Oh, the body will grow older, but God's tree only gets stronger with the passing years. Think of this the next time you see those tall, stately trees by the river.

Prayer

Heavenly Father, I thank you for giving me life and the ability to appreciate your world of nature. Even more, I am grateful for the new life in Christ that you have granted me, and for the privilege of drawing strength and nourishment from him. Amen.

 # IT'S NEVER TOO LATE TO START OVER

The jar that he was forming didn't turn out as he wished, so he kneaded it into a lump and started again. Jeremiah 18:4

EVEN adults can learn from object lessons.

One day God sent Jeremiah down to the potter's house to teach him an important truth. The potter placed a piece of clay upon the wheel and began manipulating it to form a vase. But in the process the vase became marred, so he crushed it in his hands and started over again. Then Jeremiah finally got the message. God is the God of new beginnings!

This illustration came alive for me when I visited Oberammergau, Germany, at the close of World War II. The man who played the part of the Cristos in the world famous passion play was a potter by trade and my host for an afternoon. He took me into his shop and demonstrated his art. He took some clay, threw it upon a flat disc, and turned it by means of an old pre-war Singer sewing machine treadle. Right in the middle of his demonstration, he scooped the unfinished vase off the disc, crushed it into a ball, and started over. I asked why he did this, and he explained that the clay was not "responsive." My German jeep driver explained that the clay was not pliable enough, for some dirt had gotten into the mixture.

The lesson hardly needs any explanation, it is so transparent. Just as the potter takes the marred, hardened, unresponsive clay and starts over, so God is the God of new beginnings. The entire history of the Bible, and especially the stories about the people of Israel, testifies to that truth. God only gives up on those who have given up on him. "When they gave God up and would not even acknowledge him, God gave them up" (Rom. 1:28).

But for those who receive the Lord, and acknowledge him as Lord and Savior, there is the opportunity for a fresh start. Jesus called it a "new birth" (John 3:3). When we were marred and unresponsive because of our sins, the Holy Spirit breathed upon us, and we became newly born children of God.

It is likewise true for those who have known the Lord, but who have drifted away. The Lord is willing to forgive and to start all over. This is called revival, for it is the rekindling of life. There are many Christians whose whole life seems to have disintegrated, their dreams and plans have been shattered. The grand truth is that the Master Potter stands ready to take your marred life and begin again.

No matter how old we are, it is never too late to start **over**.

Prayer

Dear Lord, thank you for not giving up on me. I want my life to be like clay in the hands of the potter. "Mold me and make me after thy will, while I am waiting, yielded and still." Amen.

ESCAPING TEMPTATION'S POWER

No temptation is irresistible. You can trust God to keep the temptation from becoming so strong that you can't stand up against it, for he has promised this and will do what he says. He will show you how to escape temptation's power so that you can bear up patiently against it.
1 Corinthians 10:13

THERE is a significant difference between temptation and testing. Although the same word is used for both in the original manuscripts, the context usually determines which English word is appropriate. Temptation is always used in the negative sense in Scripture in connection with evil. This is why James says, "God cannot be tempted with evil." So, when the comedian says, "The Devil made me do it," he is theologically correct.

Testing, on the other hand, is almost always used in the positive sense, for constructive purposes. Automobile companies spend fortunes subjecting their cars to all kinds of torturous tests, in order to produce a stronger, more dependable product. And this is God's purpose also. For example, Genesis 22:1 says that "God tested Abraham." Abraham met the test and came out a stronger man.

We can be very sure that the testings from God and the temptations from Satan will always be with us.

We will never outgrow them. So, when the times of testing come, we must accept them with patience and confidence, knowing that our loving Father wants to produce a stronger and better product. And when the times of temptation come, we should look to Jesus for our example, for he also was tempted. And like Jesus, we must claim the promises of God. He responded to each temptation by an appeal to the authority of the Word of God.

And what is the promise of God's Word to us in our temptations? "You can trust God to keep the temptation from becoming so strong that you can't stand up against it."

Prayer

Gracious Lord, I praise you for showing me how to escape the strong power of temptation in my life. Like my Savior, I want to be victorious over Satan. I confess my need of your strength. Amen.

# THE SPIRIT'S
SEAL UPON US

The Spirit's seal upon us means that God has already purchased us and that he guarantees to bring us to himself. Ephesians 1:14

THE matter of buying and selling property is no problem to a real estate broker. But to many of us who have never had occasion to buy houses and lands, it can be a monumental hassle. When we retired several years ago, we moved to Florida and bought a condominium apartment. I was totally unprepared for the stack of papers that needed to be signed. I was beginning to get writer's cramp just writing my name. And then the papers had to be signed by witnesses and impressed with an official seal.

I thought to myself, there must be an easier way of transferring property from one owner to another. Then I happened to read Jeremiah 32, and realized that it was just as complicated in the "good old days" as it is today. In thinking further about it, I even began to be grateful for all the hassle, for it was all done for my benefit. I had irrefutable proof that the property was mine.

Paul takes this illustration of sealing the title deed and applies it to God's purchase of lost humanity. To make the transaction official, it was validated by the

Holy Spirit, who placed his seal upon us. But before he could do this, the price had to be paid. In 1 Corinthians 6:20 and 7:23, Paul says "You have been bought and paid for by Christ, so you belong to him."

Jesus paid the supreme price for us by giving up his own life. He took our own sins upon himself, so that we might be forgiven, cleansed, and presented to the Father as a holy possession. Therefore, Paul concludes, we ought to "glorify God."

A seal itself has no intrinsic power. Power lies in the authority it represents. The seal of the Spirit upon Christ's purchased possession, the church, is symbolic of the power of God's invincible kingdom. It is God's witness to the world that we belong to him. We have been signed, sealed, and delivered. The hymn writer said:

'Tis done! The great transaction's done!
I am my Lord's, and he is mine.

Prayer

Dear Father, I praise you for the assurance of your love. You have not only redeemed me, but you have guaranteed that someday you will bring me to yourself. I want to glorify you with my life. Amen.

 # WORDLESS PRAYERS

The Holy Spirit prays for us with such feeling that it cannot be expressed in words. Romans 8:26

MOST of us can identify with Paul when he voices his own frustration with prayer. "We don't even know what we should pray for, nor how to pray as we should" (v. 26). God is aware of our predicament, and has graciously provided the solution. Twice in Romans 8:24–27 we are told that the Holy Spirit comes to our rescue and articulates our deepest needs and thoughts.

First, he assures us that the Spirit intercedes for us at the emotional level. "The Holy Spirit prays for us with such feeling that it cannot be expressed in words." This indicates a depth of emotion that is inexpressible. One of the most difficult calls I ever made as a pastor was upon an older couple, to break the news to them that their only son, his wife, and their three children had been burned to death. After informing them of the tragedy, we sat down together in tearful silence. The father tried several times to speak, but his voice failed him. We were all too emotionally spent to pray. And yet, after a little while we all felt an overwhelming sense of release. We knew that God had heard our inarticulate cries.

The hymn writer James Montgomery had this in mind when he wrote:

> *Prayer is the soul's sincere desire,*
> *Unuttered or expressed;*
> *The motion of a hidden fire*
> *That trembles in the breast.*
>
> *Prayer is the burden of a sigh,*
> *The falling of a tear,*
> *The upward glancing of an eye*
> *When none but God is near.*

The second time Paul mentions the Spirit's praying for us, it is at the intellectual level: ". . . he pleads for us in harmony with God's own will" (v. 27). Prayer is more than an emotional cry to God, it is an appeal for intelligent counsel.

When we are facing important, life-changing decisions, the Holy Spirit presents our needs to the Father with perfect knowledge of the Father's will. This lifts our prayer out of the realm of pure emotion, or even speculation, and conforms it to the perfect will of God. I might pray for the wrong thing, but the Holy Spirit cannot ask anything for me that would be contrary to his will for my life.

Prayer

Gracious Holy Spirit, thank you for taking my wordless prayers and presenting them to the Father, and for interpreting my needs, even though I cannot express them. Amen.

M u s i n g s . . .

It is the response of the one being taught that determines whether or not change and growth takes place. Susan T. Stevenson

Earth breaks up, time drops away,
In flows heaven, with its new day
Of endless life, when He who trod,
Very man and very God,
This Earth in weakness, shame and pain,
Dying the death whose signs remain
Up yonder on the accursed tree—
Shall come again, no more to be
Of captivity the thrall,
But the one God, All in all,
King of kings and Lord of lords,
As his servant John received the words,
"I died, and live forevermore!"
Robert Browning
From "Christmas Eve"

We must always change, renew, rejuvenate our-selves; otherwise we harden. Goethe

The truest end of life is to know the Life that never ends. William Penn

WHIRRING WHEELS
Lord, when on my bed I lie,
  Sleepless, unto Thee I cry;

When my brain works overmuch,
  Stay the wheels with Thy soft touch.

Just a quiet thought of Thee,
  And of Thy sweet charity,
Just a little prayer, and then
  I will turn to sleep again.
John Oxenham

To me prayer is "come-apart time" so that I
won't come apart emotionally and mentally
because of the pressure of daily living.
Millie Dienert

But his delight is in the law of the Lord, and on
his law he meditates day and night.
Psalm 1:2 (RSV)

Create in me a new, clean heart, O God, filled
with clean thoughts and right desires.
Psalm 51:10

OPPORTUNITIES

GOD HAS GIVEN EACH OF US THE ABILITY TO DO CERTAIN THINGS WELL. . . . IF YOUR GIFT IS THAT OF SERVING OTHERS, SERVE THEM WELL. IF YOU ARE A TEACHER, DO A GOOD JOB OF TEACHING . . . IF GOD HAS GIVEN YOU MONEY, BE GENEROUS IN HELPING OTHERS WITH IT . . . THOSE WHO OFFER COMFORT TO THE SORROWING SHOULD DO SO WITH CHRISTIAN CHEER. DON'T JUST PRETEND THAT YOU LOVE OTHERS: REALLY LOVE THEM. Romans 12:6-9

THE CHURCH DOORMAN

I would rather be a doorman of the Temple of my God than live in palaces of wickedness.
Psalm 84:10

THE man who ushered us to our seat was a friendly, cheerful person with a warm smile. He was sincere without being solicitous. It was our first visit to that church, and we felt genuinely welcomed. Some time later I learned that our friendly usher was a retired minister. He had served several large churches during his long ministry, and had moved to this small community for his retirement years. From time to time he filled the pulpit for vacationing pastors, but he obviously enjoyed his service as an usher.

This was a tremendous inspiration to me, as well as a revelation. I have known many pastors over the years of my ministry, but I can't think of many who would be humble enough to be "a doorkeeper in the house of God." I've vowed that I would be willing to do whatever service was needed in our own church. I have since preached in the pastor's absence and have filled in for absent Sunday school teachers. But as yet there has been no vacancy in the ushers' corps. I hope I may prove worthy of such an honor, if it becomes available.

Humility is not a natural grace. That is, it is not something that is second nature to us, or something we inherit from our parents. It is the one virtue we can't brag about, for the minute we brag about it, we no longer have it. We've all heard about the pastor who was given a medal for being the most humble pastor in his denomination, but when he wore it, they revoked it.

Andrew Murray was right on target when he defined humility as, "Simply acknowledging the truth of *our* position as God's creatures, and yielding to God *his* rightful place." Or, to put it even more simply, a truly humble person is one who knows himself and who knows God. To know ourselves is to be realistic about our weaknesses, imperfections and human frailty. And to know God is to recognize his infinite majesty, holiness, love, and power.

Perhaps if more of us would take the lower seat, the Lord might say, "Come up higher." "For everyone who tries to honor himself shall be humbled; and he who humbles himself shall be honored" (Luke 14:11). I hope they need an usher at my church soon!

Prayer
Pascal prayed, "Teach us, O Lord, to do little things as though they were great . . . and teach us to do the great things as though they were little." Amen.

CHEER UP

"I have told you all this so that you will have peace of heart and mind. Here on earth you will have many trials and sorrows; but cheer up, for I have overcome the world." John 16:33

HAVE you ever noticed how frequently Jesus encouraged people? One of his favorite expressions was "Cheer up." The Greek word *tharseo* means "to take courage, don't be afraid, take heart, cheer up," and it is variously translated in other translations.

The first time Jesus used that expression was in the town of Capernaum. He had been speaking to a standing room only audience in a home when he heard a noise overhead. Soon a small opening appeared, and he saw four men tearing at the roof tiles in order to enlarge the opening. Finally, when the hole was large enough, he saw them lower a young man on a stretcher before the startled eyes of everyone.

What was the very first thing Jesus said to the paralyzed boy? He said, "Cheer up, son." It was just a brief word of encouragement, but it lifted a sagging spirit at a time of desperate need.

Among the many gifts of the Spirit listed in Romans 12:6-8 is a little known gift. It is called the gift of encouragement. Not many of us can preach, perform miracles, or practice the more spectacular gifts of the

Spirit, but the gift of encouragement is one that most of us can use. Obviously some people are more gifted in this area than others. I know Christians who can go to those who are sick and suffering, or the grief stricken, and offer a word of encouragement. Because it is a gift, they are able to say "Cheer up," without it sounding trite.

Here is a challenge for each of us today. Let us think of one person we know who is despondent and discouraged. Then let us go to that person, show love, and in the name of Jesus, say "Be of good cheer."

Prayer
Dear Lord, there are so many fearful, discouraged people around me that I hardly know where to begin. Lead me by your Holy Spirit to the person you want me to encourage, and help me to say what you would want me to say. Amen.

MAKING A SAFE INVESTMENT

I know the one in whom I trust, and I am sure that he is able to safely guard all that I have given him until the day of his return. 2 Timothy 1:12

FACING retirement means facing the matter of investments for the future. I once asked a friend, a professional investment counselor, for advice about how to invest my meager life's savings. He surprised me by asking: "What are you most interested in, profits or security?" I thought about the question and had to admit that I was more interested in the security of my investment than the size of the return. We tend to get a little more cautious as we get older.

In Paul's day they didn't have the highly sophisticated banking systems we have today. Money lending was a common business, but it wasn't conducted in the plush office buildings we find today. Neither did they have the storage areas called "vaults," where people could rent safety deposit boxes for their valuables. Consequently, people kept their money in secure places in the home. When they took a long journey it was a common practice to take their valuables to the home of a trusted friend and commit them to him for safekeeping until their return.

It is probably to this ancient custom that Paul alludes in this text. He is no doubt referring to his invaluable soul as the treasure he was entrusting to the Lord. How could he so confidently commit his eternal soul to Christ? He says, "I *know* the one in whom I trust, and I am *sure* that he is able to safely guard all that I have given him." The basis for such commitment is trust.

We frequently read about people who lost their entire life's savings because of a reluctance to trust the bank. Up to this point my investment has been safe. It hasn't produced as much income as a riskier investment might, but I have peace about it.

More importantly, I have never regretted the decision I made many years ago to commit my greatest treasure, my eternal soul, into the hands of my Lord and Savior.

Prayer

Dear Lord Jesus, you have said that my eternal soul is more valuable than anything in all the world. I want to entrust my soul to you. I know that you are trustworthy, and that my soul is safe. Amen.

RELIABLE GUIDES

I am but a pilgrim here on earth: how I need a map—and your commands are my chart and guide. Psalm 119:19

I take a great deal of ribbing from my friends who are aware of my atrocious sense of direction. They express wonder that I, who have been a licensed pilot for over thirty years, have a hard time finding my way out of a supermarket. They are amused that I have a compass mounted on the dashboard of my car and that the glove compartment is overflowing with all kinds of maps.

Charts, maps and compasses might seem a little prosaic in this age of advanced navigational technology, but they still perform much-needed functions.

In our text, David refers to his need for a map, and then concludes that God's commands are sufficient. It is true that the Word of God is still the best navigational aid for the Christian.

In Psalm 119:105 David says, "Your words are a flashlight to light the path ahead of me, and keep me from stumbling." Throughout the Scriptures we have instructions concerning how to live and reliable principles on which to base our decisions. These instructions have been given to help us, not restrict us. They steer us around the pitfalls and dangerous crevices, and enable us to walk in the right direction.

Then, in addition to the reliable guide called the Bible, God has given us his Holy Spirit. Jesus said that when the Holy Spirit comes, he will guide you "into all truth" (John 16:13). Indeed, Paul made this a mark of the true Christian when he wrote, "For all who are led by the Spirit of God are sons of God" (Rom. 8:14). This awareness of the daily leading of the Holy Spirit is something every Christian can enjoy. We ought to begin each day by thanking the Lord that he has provided us with such a reliable guide.

A third reliable guide is the counsel and wisdom of godly Christian men and women. Not that their counsel is infallible, but that their wisdom comes from many years of experience. As I look back over the years of my pilgrimage, I think of scores of spiritual men and women who helped me make many important decisions. In fact, it was a spiritually perceptive professor of Bible, Edith Torrey, who first encouraged me to consider the pastoral ministry. How true are the following words of meditation:

Prayer
Precious promise God has given
To the weary passerby,
All the way from earth to heaven
I will guide thee with mine eye.

Thank you, God. Amen.

HOW TO BUILD A STONE ALTAR

Each of you is to carry out a stone on your shoulder—twelve stones in all, one for each of the twelve tribes. We will use them to build a monument so that in the future, when your children ask, "What is this monument for?" you can tell them. Joshua 4:5-7

THE atmosphere was electric with excitement! Israel was on the move to the Land of Promise, and nothing could stop them. They had camped at the shore of the Jordan for three days and now it was time for God to act. Carrying the Ark of God upon their shoulders, the priests stepped into the muddy river and the waters parted. They walked to the middle of the river, then paused while the entire host of Israel passed through. At this point, God instructed twelve men to pick up twelve stones from the middle of the riverbed and carry them to the Jericho side and there build an altar. The altar of stones was to serve as a perpetual reminder to succeeding generations of the miraculous deliverance by God.

In a similar manner, those of us who are older are responsible for erecting an altar of remembrance for those who come after us. Then, when they ask, "What is this monument for?" it can be said, "This is to be a permanent reminder that our God is a living God, who has opened up impossible paths for us."

Of course, our altar will not be made of literal

143

stones. But it will consist of those foundational principles that are eternal. In building such an altar, we need to select our stones carefully. At the very base should be the stone of faith in Jesus Christ. There should be a stone of confidence in the Holy Scriptures. Another ought to be a stone of faith in the sovereign guidance of God. The altar should also contain a stone of consistent prayer, as well as one representing dedicated service. It should include a stone representing the ministry of the Holy Spirit. Then, the keystone of the entire altar needs to be the stone of love. Future generations need to be reminded that love is the only thing that can bring peace, reconciliation, understanding, and justice to our troubled world.

It is not too late to begin work on a monument to God's grace. Let us rise up and build.

Prayer
Heavenly Father, you have led us for many years, often through difficult paths, but always with love and mercy. I am grateful for the Christians of a former generation, who took the time to raise their spiritual altars in order that we might pause to remember your loving grace. Amen.

 # GOD DOESN'T WASTE ANYTHING

"Gather the scraps," Jesus told his disciples, "so that nothing is wasted." And twelve baskets were filled with the leftovers! John 6:12, 13

IT was a long, hot day in Palestine. All afternoon the people sat entranced as the Lord of glory unfolded eternal truths. This was no ordinary twenty-minute sermonette, but a Bible-teaching of great substance. Yet, no one seemed concerned about the time of day. Typically, it was one of the disciples who expressed a concern about Sunday dinner, and suggested that Jesus pronounce the benediction and send the hungry congregation away.

Not so with Jesus. He proceeded to make arrangements to share a few small fish and a couple of stale biscuits with the five thousand men, plus an unnumbered group of women and children. After blessing the food, they began to distribute it. And, wonder of wonders, the more they gave away, the more they had left. They ended up with twelve baskets full of leftovers.

What do you do with leftovers? The Bible doesn't say what Jesus and the disciples did with them, but knowing the compassionate nature of our Lord, he probably said, "There is a village nearby with a lot of hungry people in it. Let's take these leftovers to them, that they might also be filled."

God doesn't waste anything—it is still true today. None of our experiences is wasted. All the training we have had, and all the people we have met will be used by God in our further development.

I spent four years in college, majoring in physical education. Then the Lord abruptly and dramatically turned me in a totally different direction, and I found myself in a pastoral ministry. My first thought was, "What a waste of time and money in preparing for a life's work that God never intended!"

Time has proved the wisdom of God's choice, and the years of athletic preparation were not wasted. God used those experiences to broaden my ministry beyond the local church. I have had many opportunities to minister to high school, college, and professional athletes.

So, they gathered up the leftovers so that nothing would be wasted. What a frugal Lord we have! He will gather up each experience of our lives, even those that appear to be superfluous, and find a use for them.

Prayer
Heavenly Father, give me the faith to believe that there are no wasted experiences. There are things that have happened to me for which I have no adequate explanation. Thank you for taking these experiences of my life and placing them in your basket. Amen.

TOO COLD TO PLOW

If you won't plow in the cold, you won't eat at the harvest. Proverbs 20:4

MY first church was in a small New Hampshire village where many of the men of my congregation were farmers. I can still see them on cold spring mornings riding their tractors, plowing the still hardened soil. They were bundled in warm clothing, their breath condensing in the frosty air.

In Proverbs 20 Solomon describes a lazy farmer. (The original text calls him a "sluggard.") He rises up early on a brisk, spring morning, looks at the *Farmer's Almanac* and says, "Martha, it's time to prepare the fields for sowing." He goes out to the barn to hitch up the oxen to the plow, shivering in the cold light of dawn. In a short while he returns to the house, announces to his wife, "It is too cold to plow" and puts his feet back on the stove. But when harvesttime rolls around, he and his family go hungry.

The message of the proverb is obvious. Everything worth having costs something. If we want to eat, we must work. If we desire knowledge, we must study. If we hope to have a healthy body, we must take care of it. If we expect to have a close relationship, we must spend time at it. And if we want to share in God's harvest, we must get out and plow, in spite of any inconvenience.

The lazy farmer in the proverb didn't get the message. He wanted to plow when the conditions suited him. For the same reason I am a less than average golfer. I refuse to play golf if it is too cold, too warm, too humid, too wet, or too early in the morning.

Many of us retired Christians are like that when it comes to participating in God's work. We want to serve the Lord at our convenience. We enjoy our freedom, so we refuse to make any kind of a commitment that might tie us down. We will serve the Lord if it doesn't require any sacrifice or hardship.

But at the root of it all is the failure to see the future. The lazy farmer was more concerned about his present comfort than the future harvest. Much of our reluctance to plow in God's field is due to shortsightedness. We tend to sacrifice the eternal harvest for our temporal convenience and comfort. Like the proverbial mail carrier, neither rain, nor cold, nor heat of day should prevent us from plowing God's field, no matter what our age!

Prayer
Heavenly Father, help me to overcome a tendency toward indolence. Enable me to be willing to endure personal loss and inconvenience for the sake of your work. Amen.

THE SELF-LIFE OR THE SURRENDERED LIFE

"Anyone who keeps his life for himself shall lose it; and anyone who loses his life for me shall find it again." Matthew 16:25

Christ's words concerning keeping and losing life remind me of a true story I heard a pastor relate concerning one of his young grandsons. Billy loved his grandmother dearly, and when he heard that she was in the hospital he was very sad. Then he overheard his parents saying that his grandmother desperately needed a blood transfusion, but that her blood type was quite rare.

Billy insisted that he wanted to give his blood to save his grandmother since his was also the same type. After arrangements were made for the unusual transfusion, Billy watched apprehensively as the nurse inserted the needle into his arm. He was quite nervous and shaken during the procedure. When she was finished and had removed the needle, the young boy asked, "How soon will I die?" Suddenly the nurse realized the reason for his fear. Billy had thought that giving his blood meant giving his life, and he had been prepared to die for his grandmother.

In the very truest sense, by his willingness to lose his life for the sake of one he loved, Billy had found it again. This is precisely what Jesus had been talking to his disciples about in the above Scripture. He was contrasting the self-life with the surrendered life. The person who lives for self will someday discover that his entire life was wasted. He may have been financially successful and had everything he wanted, but in the end it will have all turned to ashes. A total loss!

On the other hand, if like Billy we offer our life in surrender to the Lord, we will be losing our claim upon it. But we will gain an infinitely better and more satisfying life. The choice is ours to make.

Prayer
Heavenly Father, I desire to yield up my life to you, but the pull of the old selfish life is very strong. I want to live for you and others. Strengthen and help me crucify the old self-life, so that I might truly live. Amen.

M u s i n g s . . .

We make our decisions, and then our decisions turn around and make us. F. W. Boreham

Faith is only worthy of the name when it erupts into action. Catherine Marshall

This I learned from the shadow of a tree
  That to and fro did sway against a wall;
Our shadow selves, our influence may fall
  Where we ourselves can never be.
A. E. Hamilton

God designed the human machine to run on Himself. He Himself is the fuel our spirits were designed to burn, or the food our spirits were designed to feed on. There isn't any other.
C. S. Lewis

Live your life while you have it. Life is a splendid gift. There is no thing small in it. For the greatest things grow by God's law out of the smallest. But to live your life you must discipline it. You must not fritter it away, but make your thoughts, your acts, all work to the same end, and that end not self but God.
Florence Nightingale

Feed on Christ, and then go and live your life, and it is Christ in you that lives your life, that helps the poor,

that tells the truth,
that fights the battle, and
that wins the crown.
Phillips Brooks

When one door closes, another opens, but we
often look so long and regretfully upon the closed
door, we do not see the ones which open for us.
Alexander Graham Bell

The older I grow—and I now stand on the brink
of eternity—the more comes back to me that sen-
tence in the Catechism which I learned when a
child, and the fuller and deeper its meaning be-
comes:
"What is the chief end of man?
To glorify God and enjoy him forever."
Thomas Carlyle

Our grand business is not to see what lies dimly
in the distance, but to do what lies clearly at
hand. Thomas Carlyle, from the *Westminster*
Catechism

Happy are all who perfectly follow the laws of
God. Happy are all who search for God, and al-
ways do his will, rejecting compromise with evil,
and walking only in his paths. You have given
us your laws to obey—oh, how I want to follow
them consistently. Psalm 119:1-4

And whatever you do or say, let it be as a repre-
sentative of the Lord Jesus. Colossians 3:17

MEDITATIONS

HOPE

YET THERE IS ONE RAY OF HOPE:
HIS COMPASSION NEVER ENDS. IT
IS ONLY THE LORD'S MERCIES
THAT HAVE KEPT US FROM COM-
PLETE DESTRUCTION. GREAT IS HIS
FAITHFULNESS; HIS LOVINGKIND-
NESS BEGINS AFRESH EACH DAY.
MY SOUL CLAIMS THE LORD AS MY
INHERITANCE; THEREFORE I WILL
HOPE IN HIM. THE LORD IS WON-
DERFULLY GOOD TO THOSE WHO
WAIT FOR HIM, TO THOSE WHO
SEEK FOR HIM. IT IS GOOD BOTH
TO HOPE AND WAIT QUIETLY FOR
THE SALVATION OF THE LORD.
Lamentations 3:21-26

WHO'S IN CHARGE HERE?

And God has put all things under his [Christ's] feet, and made him the supreme Head of the church. Ephesians 1:22

I was sitting by the swimming pool one afternoon, eavesdropping on a conversation occurring at a table nearby. Several people were engaged in a heated controversy over a movie they had seen the night before. I didn't get the name of the movie, because it's hard to eavesdrop when your ears are plugged with water.

Evidently the movie dealt with the subject of the ultimate takeover of the world by alien forces. Three of the people involved were quite agitated and downright fearful that the thesis of the movie could be right, and that we were in imminent danger of being overthrown by this unknown evil empire from space. The lone member of the opposition party was just as convinced that it was an impossible fantasy.

Since these people were all in their sixties or seventies, and apparently well educated, I couldn't write them off as youthful dreamers. After they had left, I sat there thinking about the future.

The statements of Scripture concerning who is really in charge of the world and its future came to me. I began to reread the first chapter of Ephesians. There

I read again those reassuring words concerning God raising Christ from the dead, "and seated him in the place of honor at God's right hand in heaven, far, far above any other king or ruler or dictator or leader. . . . And God has put all things under his feet" (Eph. 1:20-22).

The area of Christ's control is universal. The "all things under his feet" implies universal control over all material worlds, all people and nations, and all spiritual powers. It it true that there are evil forces abroad in our world, but the Bible assures us of their ultimate defeat.

So the next time you are sitting by the pool, listening to people discussing the future of our world, you can remind them that God is still running the store, and that he has already determined how it will all end. The very last book of the Bible declares, "The kingdom of this world now belongs to our Lord, and to his Christ; and he shall reign forever and ever" (Rev. 11:15).

There's hope, because he's in charge!

Prayer
Strong Son of God, King of Kings and Lord of Lords, I worship you. The future holds no terrors for me, for you are in control. Thank you for your promise to create new heavens and a new earth where righteousness will dwell. Amen.

# WHO CAN I TURN TO?

"Master, to whom shall we go? You alone have the words that give eternal life." John 6:68

THE pathetic plight of the person without the Lord is epitomized in the popular love song, "Who can I turn to if you turn away?" The words have a common resemblance to Peter's question, "To whom shall we go?" In other words, what are the alternatives? If we do not turn to Christ in our hour of deepest need, to whom then can we turn?

Peter's question was prompted by a question the Lord had asked several of his followers. He had been speaking about some very deep and mysterious subjects relating to their partaking of his flesh and blood. At this point, several of them had started edging toward the exit. Jesus stopped them short with the question, "Are you going to walk out on me too?"

Suddenly it dawned on Peter that if he and his friends turned away from Jesus, they would have nowhere to go, and no one else to turn to. So Peter replied with a question of quiet resignation, "Master, to whom shall we go? You alone have the words that give eternal life."

What are the alternatives to following Christ?

Where else can we turn in order to find a meaningful explanation for life? Philosophy, science, and education are helpful, but education without God is like a man without a soul, or a ship without a rudder.

Where can we go to obtain peace of mind and heart, if not to the Lord who said, "My peace I give to you"? To whom can we turn for the answer to the problems of sin, guilt, and forgiveness, if not to the "Lamb of God who takes away our sin"? Where can we go for a reliable answer to the questions concerning immortality and the eternal future, if not to the one who said, "I am the Resurrection and the Life"?

And where can we turn for comfort and assurance in the time of our deepest sorrow and grief? Recently the husband of one of our neighbors died very suddenly. When I talked with her, she said, "I don't know what people do in times like this if they don't have the Lord!"

Peter was right, the alternatives are extremely limited.

Prayer
Lord Jesus, I am grateful that you are with me, in the good times as well as the bad. It comforts me to know that I can turn to you when I am perplexed, or when my heart is bowed down with sorrow. Thank you for your loving concern and compassion. Amen.

THE LIVING SAVIOR

"But as for me, I know that my Redeemer lives, and that he will stand upon the earth at last. And I know that after this body has decayed, this body shall see God." Job 19:25, 26

ARTHUR BRISBANE, a noted columnist of several generations ago, wrote a fascinating little story. He told about some forest creatures who had found a dried caterpillar cocoon clinging to a branch. They all expressed their sorrow over the fact that the little caterpillar had not had a decent burial. So they set about to prepare for its funeral.

As the forest creatures were in the process of conducting the funeral service, they were bothered by a persistent butterfly that kept flitting frantically around their heads. Unknown to them, this was the creature they thought they were burying. It had emerged from its temporary cocoon and was very much alive.

The story becomes a living parable. When they had laid Jesus in the tomb, everyone assumed that this was the final chapter. Yet, even while they were in the process of burying him, he reappeared in his new, glorified body.

And so shall it be with each of God's children. Job spoke the truth when he said, "my Redeemer lives." We do not worship a Savior whose body lies somewhere in a Palestinian tomb. We worship and serve a living Savior, One who not only "died for our sins according to the scriptures; [but] was buried, and . . . rose again the third day according to the scriptures" (1 Cor. 15:3,4, KJV).

This is the heart of our faith, for without the Resurrection there would be no hope, and no future, and we would be, of all people, most miserable. Can you say with the assurance of Job, "As for me, I know that my Redeemer lives"?

Prayer

Dear Father, you are the living God, and your Son Jesus is our Resurrection and Life. In the midst of a dying world, we thank you for such a dynamic hope. Amen.

TRUE AND FALSE HOPE

I pray that God will help you overflow with hope in him through the Holy Spirit's power within you. Romans 15:13

THERE is a big difference between a true hope and one that is false. A true hope is one that is confident of fulfillment, while a false hope has no such expectation. A true hope is one that is rooted in the promises of God, but a false hope is founded on unwarranted optimism. A true hope is one that produces satisfaction, while a false hope only ensures disappointment. In Romans 5:5 Paul spoke about "a hope that does not disappoint us" (NIV).

A false hope is one that is unrealistic and unattainable. I might hope to wake up tomorrow morning looking like a trim, young, curly-haired athlete, but that is an unrealistic hope. Instead, I'm afraid that I'll wake up looking like the bald, paunchy, over sixty-five that I am. Some of us ex-athletes have now reached the stage where weight lifting consists of just standing up! An unrealistic hope will always disappoint.

Hope can also prove to be disappointing if its object is unworthy. A recent winner of a million dollar lottery said, "It is something I have hoped for all my life!" Yet, just six months later he described his good fortune as a "disaster." He has been plagued by visitors, phone calls, solicitors, and people who want to help him spend the money. "I don't even know who my friends are anymore," he said bitterly.

On the other hand, the Bible describes the Christian's hope as "living, steadfast, unashamed, saving, joyful, abounding, glorious and blessed." And above all, it is certain of fulfillment, because it is based upon God's sure and certain promises. We have the promised hope of God's providential care, of the glorious return of Christ, of an abundant entrance into heaven and eternal life. Because our hope is in God, we confidently expect to realize his every promise.

Let us bid good-bye to wishful thinking, and say hello to biblical hope.

Prayer

My hope, blessed Jesus, is anchored in Thee,
Thy righteousness only now covereth me;
Thy blood, shed on Calvary, now is my plea;
My hope, my hope is in Thee. Amen.

 # IN SPITE OF EVERYTHING

Even though the fig trees are all destroyed, and there is neither blossom left nor fruit, and though the olive crops all fail, and the fields lie barren; even if the flocks die in the fields and the cattle barns are empty, yet I will rejoice in the Lord; I will be happy in the God of my salvation.
Habakkuk 3:17, 18

CROP failures, dead fruit orchards, diminished flocks and herds—a hypothetical agricultural disaster of great proportions. In this ancient text God's prophet expressed his confidence that even if such a catastrophe should occur, he would not lose faith.

Since not all of us have been farmers, let me broaden Habakkuk's rural illustration to include the rest of us. It could read like this, "Though my business fails, and though I may suffer sickness, and even face heartbreaking sorrow, yet I will continue to trust in the goodness and mercy of God." (You may add to this your own list of hypothetical possibilities.)

How can we, like Habakkuk, so confidently say that we will continue to rejoice in the Lord, even if we arc faced with such distress? We can be confident because our faith in the goodness of God does not depend upon our prosperity or lack of it. Neither is it dependent upon our health or loss of it. Nor is it dependent upon our suffering or freedom from it.

God never promised to keep us immune from the ordinary trials of life just because we are Christians.

He *has* promised to sustain us, bless us, and strengthen us in the midst of our trials. Therefore, it is possible for us to endure hardship without being destroyed by it. And it is possible to experience trials without becoming angry, resentful, or full of self-pity. That is what Job meant when he cried out, "Though he slay me, yet will I trust in him" (Job 13:15, KJV). It is another way of saying, "In spite of everything, I will rejoice in the Lord."

Prayer
Heavenly Father, even though I do not always understand why you allow certain problems to come my way, give me the faith to believe that even these hardships can make me strong. Amen.

# IS YOUR ANCHOR DRAGGING?

This certain hope of being saved is a strong and trustworthy anchor for our souls, connecting us with God. Hebrews 6:19

AN anchor has only one purpose—to keep the boat from drifting into unwanted areas. As a boy, I spent many summers in a small Pennsylvania town on the Susquehanna River. One day a friend and I took a boat out on the river, threw over our homemade anchor, a large stone tied with a rope, and then stretched out to enjoy the sun. We became drowsy and soon fell asleep. Unknown to us, the rope holding our makeshift anchor became loose, and we drifted almost twenty-five miles downstream. Very frightened when we awakened, we quickly learned the value of a "strong and trustworthy anchor."

In this life there is very little that is secure. It is possible to lose our jobs, homes, investments, health, and everything we depend on for our present and future security. The storms of economic uncertainty, the clouds of potential war, and the winds of political instability can cause the ship to drift. It is for these reasons that we need a strong, dependable anchor, one that will dig deep into the ocean floor and hold our ship steady.

We Christians face the same storms that confront other people. We are affected by the same concerns, the same sicknesses, the same sorrows, for we are a part of the same fallen world. But because we are part of God's family there is an overwhelming difference. As the text says, because we have a certain hope of being saved, we have "a strong and trustworthy anchor for our souls, connecting us with God." And because of this unfailing anchor, we can lie down in peace. As the hymn writer so graphically put it:

We have an anchor that keeps the soul,
  Steadfast and sure while the billows roll.
Fastened to the Rock, which cannot move,
  Grounded firm and deep in the Savior's love.

Prayer
Thank you Lord, for giving me something to hold on to today, and a hope for tomorrow that is a strong and trustworthy anchor. Amen.

YOU ARE GOING TO BE RICH

His Holy Spirit speaks to us deep in our hearts, and tells us that we really are God's children. And since we are his children, we will share his treasures. Romans 8:16, 17

DRIVING down the interstate highway on our way to Florida and our new life of retirement, we were passed by a beautiful, large travel home. It was complete with TV antenna, two-way radio, and auxiliary air-conditioner. Two small Honda mopeds were strapped to the front, and a brand new Dodge convertible (with sticker price still intact) was towed behind. But what really caught our attention was a prominent bumper sticker which read, "We are spending our children's inheritance."

That approach may be popular with many parents in today's world, but it is not true of our heavenly Parent. Romans 8:17 promises, ". . . since we are his [God's] children, we will share his treasures." The word translated "treasures" in *The Living Bible,* is from *kleros* meaning "a portion, or an inheritance." Since I have never inherited anything, I am looking forward to my heavenly inheritance.

Our future inheritance is mentioned more than thirty times in the New Testament. What will my inheritance be?

For one thing, I will inherit eternal life. I "will not perish, but have everlasting life" (see John 3:16). And, since "flesh and blood cannot inherit the kingdom of God," I will inherit a new body that is fitted for everlasting life in God's kingdom. It will be a body that will not deteriorate, will not experience pain or suffering, and will be perfect in every detail. Furthermore, God's Word promises there are things prepared for us which our human eyes could not see nor our ears hear. Because we are members of God's family, we are all going to be rich beyond our wildest dreams.

Prayer
Dear Father, the thought of an eternal life to enjoy the fruits of our inheritance is too staggering for my mind to understand. Thank you for including me in your family. Amen.

REWARDS THAT LAST

To win the contest you must deny yourselves many things that would keep you from doing your best. An athlete goes to all this trouble just to win a blue ribbon or a silver cup, but we do it for a heavenly reward that never disappears.
1 Corinthians 9:25

DURING my senior year in high school I won a coveted gold medal as the Pennsylvania state champion quarter-miler. The years passed and my gold medal tarnished, so I put it in a shoe box, along with some other athletic mementos. A number of years later, not realizing the sentimental value of the medal, my five-year-old son traded it for a used Mickey Mouse watch. I couldn't help but think of the humor of the situation. A tarnished gold medal for a cheap Mickey Mouse watch! Ironically, if I had the watch today, its value as a collector's item would far surpass the value of the gold-plated medal.

In 1 Corinthians 9 Paul refers to a perishable reward, one that will tarnish and disappear like my medal. In Paul's time Olympic champions received a wreath woven from laurel branches. In a short time the cherished wreath was a dry and withered reward. Paul contrasts that faded wreath with the indestructible rewards that God promises to his victorious followers.

The Bible mentions five victory rewards. The first

is a reward for self-discipline (1 Cor. 9:25). There is also a reward for those who minister in Christ's name (1 Pet. 5:2-4). A third reward is promised to those who patiently await the Lord's return (2 Tim. 4:8). There is still another reward—a crown for those who have been involved in bringing others to Christ (1 Thess. 2:19). And then there is the crown of life promised to those who triumph over temptation (Jas. 1:12).

The promises in God's Word make it clear that the Lord rewards us according to the quality of our life and service. It isn't too late to start training for the real Olympics.

Prayer
Father, help me to serve you well, not for any earthly reward, but for the heavenly. Let me serve you with true compassion. Amen.

# ONE DAY
NEARER HOME

The night is far gone, the day of his return will soon be here. Romans 13:12

WORLD WAR II was over, and I was on a ship returning home to my wife and family. The journey seemed interminable, and each day found me saying to myself, "One day nearer home!" The anticipation was almost more than I could bear.

I have never been able to understand why many Christians consider the subject of our approaching "home going" as morbid and painful to contemplate. Paul spoke about our departure to be with Christ, as "better yet" (Phil. 1:21). He also assured us that to leave the body is to be "at home" with the Lord (2 Cor. 5:8).

If those concepts are true, and we know they are, then why are we so reluctant to talk about death? One of the reasons, of course, is the human factor. None of us enjoys separations, even for a limited time. At this point our human emotions come into conflict with our theological convictions. We know in our hearts that the believing dead are in a far better and happier state than we could ever dream, yet there is the understandable grief we feel at the departure of friends and loved ones. However, as Paul says, we do not experience the same sorrow as "those who have no hope" (1 Thess. 4:13).

Death is a reality of our human condition. By looking at the positive side of this ultimate experience we can begin to plan for it, and to be ready when the Lord calls. This removes the element of fear from the subject, and frees us to face the future with confidence. The Bible promises that God "will deliver those who through fear of death have been living all their lives as slaves to constant dread" (Heb. 2:15).

In the above text, Paul reminds us that each day brings us nearer home. At summer camp we used to sing a chorus around the camp fire, at the close of each day:

Just one day nearer home,
  when shadows of the night descend;
Just one day left to roam,
  when evening twilight colors blend.
Beneath the starry dome,
  I rest beside my guide and friend;
With each day's tramping, nightly camping,
  I'm one day nearer home.

Prayer
Dear Lord, free me from any doubts about my eternal future. Help me to look forward with joy to my eternal life with you. Amen.

SEARCHING FOR THE RIGHT CITY

Abraham . . . was confidently waiting for God to bring him to that strong heavenly city whose designer and builder is God. Hebrews 11:10

WHEN my wife and I first faced the prospect of retirement, the logical question was, "Where?"

I've discovered that's a common dilemma among retirees. Children have established their homes in scattered parts of the country. Then there are the questions of: Country or city? North or south? East or west? But finally the decision is made and new beginnings are made.

We're not asking "Where?" about our future home. We know it will be in a city. Heaven is described as a city foursquare and symbolically beautiful with streets of gold and walls of jasper.

When Charles Spurgeon was asked why he was more interested in his eternal home than in his temporal one, he replied, "In asking the question you have answered it. I am more interested in my eternal home because it is eternal. Less interested in my temporal home because it is temporal." He was right, our earthly homes are temporary.

No matter where we live, Christian retirees have two homes: one temporary, one a future permanent home. The writer of Hebrews describes the situation, "For this world is not our home; we are looking forward to our everlasting home in heaven" (see Heb. 11:13-15).

There are those who say Christians are "other worldly" and "impractical dreamers." There may be some truth in such accusations, so we need to read on in Hebrews 11 and take the instructions for our earthly day by day living seriously.

What should the Christian be doing? "With Jesus' help we will continually offer our sacrifice of praise to God by telling others of the glory of his name. Don't forget to do good and share with those in need, for such sacrifices are very pleasing to him" (Heb. 13:15, 16).

Our days on earth are happier days when we reach out to others.

Prayer
With the poet and songwriter, Ira B. Wilson, I pray,

> *Make me a blessing,*
> *Out of my life may Jesus shine.*
> *Make me a blessing,*
> *O Savior, I pray.*
> *Make me a blessing to someone today. Amen.*

# WHO SAID JESUS IS COMING AGAIN?

"There are many homes up there where my Father lives, and I am going to prepare them for your coming. When everything is ready, then I will come and get you, so that you can always be with me where I am." John 14:2, 3

WHO said Jesus is coming again? Jesus did. Not only once but on numerous occasions Jesus spoke of when he would come back again.

One time, when the high priest was questioning Jesus about his claim to be the Messiah, Jesus said, "In the future you will see me, the Messiah, . . . returning on the clouds of heaven (Matt. 26:64).

Again, when Jesus was talking with his disciples about signs of the end of the age, he explained, "Then the peoples of the earth shall see me, the Messiah, coming in a cloud with power and great glory. So when all these things begin to happen, stand straight and look up! For your salvation is near" (Luke 21:27).

And during the week before his Crucifixion, when Jesus was preparing his disciples for the difficult days ahead, he said, "Let not your heart be troubled. You are trusting God, now trust in me. . . . When everything is ready, then I will come and get you, so that you can always be with me where I am" (John 14:1–3).

Then after the Crucifixion and Resurrection, and

after Jesus had talked with his followers at different times giving them convincing proof that he was alive, there came the day when they were together at the Mount of Olives and Jesus rose into the sky and disappeared into a cloud. The people stared after him, straining their eyes for another glimpse and "Suddenly two white-robed men were standing there among them, and said, 'Men of Galilee, why are you standing here staring at the sky? Jesus has gone away to heaven, and some day, just as he went, he will return!'" (Acts 1:9-11).

I can remember the first time I heard that promise of hope. As a young teenager and a new Christian, I was startled one Sunday to hear the pastor say, "Jesus is coming again." He announced it with such positive joy and conviction I thought he meant at that moment. I looked around, almost expecting Jesus to come down the aisle. From that day to this I have never been able to shake that awesome feeling of expectation each time I hear a message or a song about the Lord's return.

I join with Paul in his joyful expectation when he writes to Titus about his blessed hope, "Looking forward to that wonderful time we've been expecting, when his glory shall be seen—the glory of our great God and Savior Jesus Christ" (Titus 2:13).

Prayer
Lord, you are the King of Kings, and Lord of Lords. My heart is filled with praise whenever I think of your triumphant return. I do look forward to that wonderful time. Amen.

LOVING THE UNSEEN SAVIOR

You love him even though you have never seen him; though not seeing him, you trust him; and even now you are happy with the inexpressible joy that comes from heaven itself. 1 Peter 1:8

PETER wrote these words to a scattered group of Christians who had suffered under the persecutions of the mad emperor, Nero. They had been driven from their homes, families, and native land because of their faith in Jesus. Peter praised them for their steadfast love, their unshakeable trust, and their inexpressible joy. And the most remarkable thing of all was that not one of these people had ever seen Christ. For by that time Jesus had already ascended to the Father.

We, like those Christians of the first century, have never seen Christ. But that does not prevent us from loving and trusting him, or from being filled with inexpressible joy, thankful that we belong to him.

Years ago I saw a living illustration of an unseen love. A man who had been blinded as a child received Jesus as his Lord and Savior, and soon united with our church. In time he became acquainted with and began to show an interest in a lady from our congregation, and their friendship blossomed into marriage. At the reception following the ceremony, I approached the couple in the receiving line and identified myself. As my friend tightly held his wife's hand, he said: "Pastor, isn't she a beautiful bride?" Immediately I thought of Peter's words, "Whom having not seen, you love."

The hope of every Christian is that someday we shall see the Savior face to face. It was this thought that prompted Fanny Crosby, the blind hymn composer to write:

> *Face to face with Christ my Savior,*
> *Face to face—what will it be—*
> *When with rapture I behold Him,*
> *Jesus Christ who died for me?*
>
> *Face to face I shall behold Him,*
> *Far beyond the starry sky;*
> *Face to face in all His glory,*
> *I shall see Him by and by!*

Prayer

Jesus, I look forward to that time when I will no longer look through a glass darkly—that time when I will see you face to face. But I thank you, Lord, for eyes of faith that let me know you are with me every day—today, just where I am. Amen.

THE VIEW FROM A SYCAMORE TREE

Jesus told him, "This shows that salvation has come to this home today. . . . I, the Messiah, have come to search for and to save such souls as his." Luke 19:9, 10

I can never read Luke's story about Zacchaeus perching on the limb of an overhanging tree without remembering some of my boyhood experiences. Located at the right-field corner of our local baseball stadium in my hometown there were three large elm trees rising conveniently above the stadium's high wooden fence. Every Saturday afternoon, those of us kids who could not afford the twenty-five cents for a ticket would climb those trees and perch like a flock of crows throughout the entire nine innings.

But in Luke's story an event more exciting than a baseball game was taking place in Jericho. Jesus, the famed miracle worker, was passing through the city, and the street was crowded with the curious. Zacchacus, an influential businessman in Jericho, wasn't very tall and had difficulty seeing over the heads of the people along the road, so he ran ahead and vied with the local kids for a seat on an overhanging sycamore tree.

What was it that motivated that prominent, wealthy public official to humiliate himself in front of the whole town? Without doubt he was motivated by some curiosity. He had heard about Jesus, but had never seen him. However, I believe there was a deeper power at work in Zacchaeus's life, drawing him irresistibly to the Lord. His conscience was awakened by the Holy Spirit. I have a feeling that this impulsive act was the result of a growing dissatisfaction with his wicked life.

But probably an even deeper motivating force was the longing of hope. The entire population of Palestine knew that Jesus was accused of being the "friend of sinners." So Zacchaeus probably said to himself, "I wonder if the rumors are true?" The thought gave him hope, and off he ran to his balcony seat in the sycamore tree.

There are many valuable lessons in this experience. But the thing that stands out above all others is the personal quality of Jesus' love. He looked up, saw Zacchaeus, called him by name, and said, "I want to be your guest today!"

Zacchaeus responded to that love by bounding out of the tree quickly and walking proudly, if not tall, through the crowds and to his home. Yes, everything he had heard about Jesus was true—he was (and *is*) the friend of sinners!

Prayer

Lord Jesus, I am grateful that you loved me, even when I was unworthy, and that you personally invited me to receive you as my guest. Help me to see the many people like Zacchaeus around me who are lonely, alienated, and in deep need of meeting you. Amen.

Musings . . .

Faith is the expectancy of spring in the midst of a cold winter. Sharon Lee Roberts

In order to realize the worth of the anchor, we need to feel the stress of the storm.
Author Unknown

Take care of your life; and the Lord will take care of your death. George Whitefield

He liveth long who liveth well!
All other life is short and vain;
He liveth longest who can tell
Of living most for heavenly gain.
Horatius Bonar
He Liveth Long Who Liveth Well

I came from God, and I'm going back to God, and I won't have any gaps of death in the middle of my life. George MacDonald, *Mary Marston*

What can be hoped for which is not believed?
St. Augustine, *On Faith, Hope and Charity*

Life with Christ is an endless hope, without him a hopeless end. Anonymous

Eternity is the divine treasure house, and hope is the window by means of which mortals are per-

mitted to see, as through a glass darkly, the
things which God is preparing. William
Mountford

When John Wesley was asked what he would do
if he knew he were to die that night, he said that
he would eat his supper, preach at candlelight,
say his prayers, and go to bed. Anonymous

Why stay on earth except to grow?
Robert Browning

Although today He prunes my twigs with pain,
Yet doth his blood nourish and warm my root:
Tomorrow I shall put forth buds again,
And clothe myself with fruit.
Christina Rossetti

I pray for you . . . that God who gives you
hope will keep you happy and full of peace as
you believe in him. I pray that God will help
you overflow with hope in him through the Holy
Spirit's power within you. Romans 15:13

And this is the secret: that Christ in your hearts
is your only hope of glory. Colossians 1:27

May our Lord Jesus Christ himself and God our
Father, who has loved us and given us everlasting comfort and hope . . . comfort your hearts
with all comfort and help you in every good
thing you say and do. 2 Thessalonians 2:16, 17

CHANGES

CHEER UP, DON'T BE AFRAID. FOR THE LORD YOUR GOD HAS ARRIVED TO LIVE AMONG YOU. HE IS A MIGHTY SAVIOR. HE WILL GIVE YOU VICTORY. HE WILL REJOICE OVER YOU IN GREAT GLADNESS; HE WILL LOVE YOU AND NOT ACCUSE YOU. IS THAT A JOYOUS CHOIR I HEAR? NO, IT IS THE LORD HIMSELF EXULTING OVER YOU IN HAPPY SONG. Zephaniah 3:16-18

FROM START TO FINISH

I am sure that God who began the good work within you will keep right on helping you grow in his grace until his task within you is finally finished on that day when Jesus Christ returns.
Philippians 1:6

AN elderly minister had been called upon to offer the prayer at a ministers' conference. Like so many preachers, he could not resist the opportunity to expound. So he delivered a theological address to God. Nevertheless, his long prayer served a good purpose, for in it he dropped the seed of a sermon outline, which I, along with scores of others, noted. In his prayer he said, "I thank thee that thou hast commenced a good work in us, and that thou hast promised to continue it until the consummation." I immediately recognized this part of his prayer as his own paraphrase of Philippians 1:6, complete with the alliterative words, "commence, continue, and consummate."

If there is any one verse in Scripture that summarizes the whole purpose of God in salvation, it is this verse. For certainly our salvation had its commencement with God. We did not originate the idea, nor would we have been able to carry it out. The Bible clearly states that we are hopelessly lost and totally incapable of saving ourselves. "When we were utterly helpless with no way of escape, Christ came at just the right time and died for us sinners" (Rom. 5:6).

Furthermore, not only has God commenced this work of salvation in us, he is continuing to oversee it. God feels a responsibility to nurture his newly born child. "He will keep right on helping you grow."

My responsibility as a father doesn't end when the doctor comes out of the delivery room and says, "It's a boy!" Along with his mother, I must spend many years trying to help him grow up. It requires a lot of instruction, discipline, time, and a ton of tough love. It is comforting to know that God the Holy Spirit is at work in us, strengthening, correcting, and guiding.

How long will God's nurturing process continue? Paul says it will continue until the consummation. That is, until Jesus comes to take us to be with himself. The work of salvation will continue "until his task within you is finally finished on that day when Jesus Christ returns" (Phil. 1:6). How can we lose?

Prayer
Heavenly Father, it is good to know that it is not all up to me. Without your continuing support and strength I would fail miserably. But with your Holy Spirit working in me, I am confident that I will not fall. Amen.

 # DIVINE AMNESIA

I alone am he who blots away your sins for my own sake and will never think of them again.
Isaiah 43:25

AS we grow older, forgetfulness is one of life's irritations. It's a common problem and most of us learn to accept it. We joke about forgetting where we put our glasses. We keep conversation going until we can remember the name of a long time friend—then finally admit, "Your name has escaped, please forgive me."

On the other hand, remembering is also a problem. Most of us have memories of past mistakes, sins, and unhappy times. We wish we could go back and relive certain moments and make amends for wrong and hurtful things we've said and done. But as we go over and over the past we are robbed of the joy and peace God wants us to enjoy today.

At such times God's forgetfulness can be a great blessing to us. The prophet Isaiah points out that God promises to forget our sins and our transgressions when we come to him for forgiveness. He says, "I . . . will never think of them again" (Isa. 43:25). With his loving power, God deliberately erases even the memory of our wrongdoings and says he will not bring them to mind again.

God's promise to forget is liberating good news for every Christian. In 1 Corinthians 15:3 we read that when Jesus died on the cross he "died for our sins." When we accept this truth God says to us, "The books are closed. The slate has been wiped clean; those sins will never be held against you."

Since God has agreed to forgive and forget we ought to do the same. We need to ask the Lord to help us forgive those who have hurt us and to blot from our minds the remembrance of those happenings. We also need to pray for help to forgive ourselves and get on with living today.

Godly amnesia is a great help.

Prayer
Heavenly Father, I thank you for your promises to forgive and forget. Please enable me to let go of the past, to ask you for forgiveness and to accept the clean slate you offer to me. Amen.

TIME FOR A CHECKUP

Check up on yourselves. Are you really Christians? Do you pass the test? Do you feel Christ's presence and power more and more within you? Or are you just pretending to be Christians when actually you aren't at all? 2 Corinthians 13:5

MY doctor keeps insisting that I get regular check-ups. He smiles knowingly and says, "Now that you are over 65, you should be more conscientious about your annual physical examination." I always wonder if he knows something he isn't telling me. At any rate, deep in my heart I know he is right.

Paul was just as insistent that we be careful to check on our spiritual condition from time to time. In 2 Corinthians 13:5 he suggests that we examine ourselves to see if our profession of faith in Christ is real or counterfeit. One of the symptoms he asks us to check is, "Do you feel Christ's presence and power more and more within you?" Obviously, if there is no evidence of the presence of his Spirit, then we need to prayerfully receive him into our lives.

Communion provides us with an excellent time for self-examination. Scripture points out, "If anyone eats this bread and drinks from this cup of the Lord in an unworthy manner, he is guilty of sin against the body and the blood of the Lord. That is why a man should examine himself carefully before eating the bread and drinking from the cup" (1 Cor. 11:27, 28).

We know that none of us is really deserving of our salvation. As the Bible says, our salvation is a gift of God's grace. Pondering God's grace and our salvation causes us to enter into the communion service with rejoicing and gratitude.

And, as the Holy Spirit brings to our attention those areas of our lives that are displeasing to God, we have the opportunity to confess them and commit ourselves to a greater closeness to God. Unfortunately, we don't enjoy checkups, either from a doctor or our own conscience. This is because we tend to look upon them negatively rather than positively. But there are benefits. More often than not the report comes back, "You are in excellent condition."

Take my doctor's advice. You'll be glad you did.

Prayer

Dear Lord, I must confess that I don't enjoy the spiritual checkups any more than the physical ones. But I want my heart to be right, and to know that my life is all that you would have it to be. "Search me, O God, and know my heart." Amen.

SEEING THINGS OUT OF FOCUS

"I see men! But I can't see them very clearly; they look like tree trunks walking around!" Mark 8:24

NOT long ago I began to notice that the newspaper I was reading seemed to be slightly blurred. "Just a sloppy case of printing," I told myself. When it happened the second time, I decided to have my eyes checked. The doctor said, "This happens a lot to you retired people, you spend a lot more time reading now than you did when you were working. You have a mild eye strain."

As I left the doctor's office, I thought of Jesus' miracle recorded in Mark 8:22-26. People had brought a blind man to Jesus and pleaded with the Master to heal him. Jesus took the man aside, spat upon his eyes, and asked if he could see anything. The man said, "Yes, I can see people, but the image is so out of focus they resemble tree trunks." Whereupon Jesus touched the man's eyes again, ". . . and he saw everything clearly." The J. B. Phillips' translation says, "His sight came into focus."

There are a lot of fascinating questions about this two-phase miracle which we cannot deal with in this brief devotional. There are, however, several spiritual lessons we can draw from it. First, the miracle reminds us that no one sees spiritual truths distinctly all at once. For all of us, spiritual sight develops gradually. Just as newborn babies are unable to focus on specific images immediately, neither can newly born Christians understand all they see. Most of us who are older in the faith can see things today that we could not understand years ago.

Paul expressed this truth about spiritual sight in 1 Corinthians 13:11, 12: "When I was a child I spoke and thought and reasoned as a child does. But when I became a man my thoughts grew far beyond those of my childhood. . . . In the same way, we can see and understand only a little about God now . . . but someday we are going to see him in his completeness."

Second, while we are able to see God's truth better today than thirty years ago, it will not be until we are ushered into the Lord's presence that everything will come into perfect focus. Then "we shall know as we are known," and the many problems and unexplained spiritual mysteries will be revealed. Our weak sight will become clear, and everything will come into focus.

Prayer
Lord Jesus, anoint my spiritual eyes so I may see you more clearly, and that I might understand more of your Word. Amen.

 # COPING WITH DECLINING HEALTH

Dear friend, I am praying that all is well with you and that your body is as healthy as I know your soul is. 3 John 1:2

THIS greeting was addressed to Gaius, one of the leaders of a church in Asia Minor. It appears that Gaius was suffering from ill health, and that John's greeting was more than a polite "How do you do?" John seemed to be genuinely concerned about Gaius's deteriorating physical condition.

As we grow older we often become more anxious about our health. This is perfectly normal, for no one wants to have a lingering illness. There are some people, however, who tend to become neurotic about their health and literally worry themselves sick.

What can we do about the problem of declining health? The most obvious, of course, is to do everything possible to keep ourselves healthy, which includes proper food, sufficient rest, adequate exercise, and regular checkups.

But the solution is more than physical. It requires a right attitude. Included in the right attitude is the ability to accept reality. It is a proven fact of life that all things physical must, by the very laws of nature, retrogress. The older the house, the greater the possibility of electrical failures, plumbing problems, falling plaster, and rusting rainspouts. The older the automobile, the more likely it will be to require repair. The human body is no different, for like everything physical, it too is subject to the wearing of time.

But there is a wonderful spiritual dimension to the wearing out of our bodies. The biblical writers held out the hope of a new, rejuvenated body. Paul promised, "Our earthly bodies which die and decay are different from the bodies we shall have when we come back to life again, for they will never die" (1 Cor. 15:42, 43). This is something each child of God can anticipate.

We can do little about the inevitable decline of physical health, but we can look forward to the coming of Christ, who will then "take these dying bodies of ours and change them into glorious bodies like his own." You can't improve upon that. In the meantime, as John prayed for Gaius, I pray for you, "That all is well with you and that your body is as healthy as I know your soul is" (3 John 1:2).

Prayer
Father, as we all face the reality of our own humanity, help us to be strong and of good courage. And, above all, enable us to have a hope that goes beyond these few years of life upon this earth. Amen.

COPING WITH CHANGE

"Lord, in the beginning you made the earth, and the heavens are the work of your hands. They will disappear into nothingness, but you will remain forever. They will become worn out like old clothes, and some day you will fold them up and replace them. But you yourself will never change." Hebrews 1:10-12

Class reunions can be devastating! Someone has re-marked that a class reunion is an occasion where old classmates come together to see who has been falling apart. Probably the biggest falsehood expressed repeatedly during the entire evening is, "You haven't changed a bit!"

There is no need for such deception. We all know it is not true. A casual review of the high school yearbook or the family album will destroy such delusion. Or, worse yet, take a good look at the picture on your driver's license or passport.

Words from Psalm 102, quoted in Hebrews 1:10-12, remind us that we live in a physical world that is in a constant state of change. Nothing remains static except God himself.

I remember my disappointment in taking my family on a nostalgic trip to my boyhood home in Pennsylvania. I was crushed by what we saw. The old homestead had changed beyond recognition. Many of the neighboring houses had been razed, the old baseball field had become a town dump, and the downtown area was a total disaster.

What is true of the physical world is also true of every other area of our lives. Our world is even now in the throes of sociological, political, technological, and economic changes that are posing great challenges to our leaders. As we grow older we find it more difficult to cope with change.

In the midst of this uncertainty, it is comforting to know that there are still a few things that are untouched by the passing of time. For one thing, God's Word doesn't change. It has appeared in many language versions, but the message remains the same. And, as Hebrews 1:12 says, God never changes. How good it is to know we can rely upon the Lord, even though everything else in life will change.

Prayer

Lord, as I face the future I do not know what changes shall take place in my life. But whatever happens, I submit myself to your sovereign control. "O thou, who changest not, abide with me." Amen.

THE FIRST STREAKS OF GRAY

Ephraim's hair is turning gray, and he doesn't even realize how weak and old he is. Hosea 7:9

REMEMBER the trauma experienced at the discovery of those first few strands of graying hair. We called it "premature graying," because no one welcomes getting older. However, all the Grecian Formula in the world cannot stem the tide of time and the aging process.

Hosea used the common and very human experience of graying to teach a spiritual lesson. The faith of his nation was declining, and the people were losing their spiritual vitality and vision. They were growing old and complacent, and the sad part of it was, they were not even aware of it. It had crept upon them so gradually that they had not noticed it happening.

It can happen to any of us. We can grow to be old and complacent Christians. As young believers, we were full of faith and confidence, trusting in God and his Word. The expressions of our love for the Lord were meaningful. We enjoyed the worship services of the church. We reveled in the opportunities for service and witness. We were filled with spiritual excitement.

Now, if we are not careful as we grow older in the

faith, we begin to stagnate. The early joy and excitement of the Christian life starts to become a burden rather than a blessing. We tend to become more critical and less compassionate. And, like those first streaks of gray, the signs of spiritual aging will become noticeable to those around us, while we ourselves are unaware of it.

What is the solution to this unconscious spiritual decline? A fresh, daily commitment to the Lord will help us avoid the spiritual aging that is destructive to a life of faith. Opening our hearts to the Lord will allow the thrill and excitement that we knew in the early days of our faith to be restored.

Prayer
Lord, I do open my heart to you as I pray and sing,

> *Revive us again,*
> *fill each heart with thy love;*
> *May each soul be rekindled*
> *with fire from above.*
> *Hallelujah, thine the glory! Amen.*

A STRANGE AND WONDERFUL SECRET

I am telling you this strange and wonderful secret: we shall not all die, but we shall all be given new bodies! It will all happen in a moment, in the twinkling of an eye. 1 Corinthians 15:51, 52

WHO among us, having reached three score and five years or more, would not settle for a new body! A retired friend of mine complained, "Every part of my body hurts, and what doesn't hurt, doesn't work." He added dryly, "I find that my back goes out nowadays more often than I do."

So, what is the answer? There are only a few parts of our bodies that can be replaced with transplants. It is something like owning a car. After a while things begin to go wrong with it—the tires wear out, it needs a new muffler, the battery gets weak, and the transmission starts to make odd noises. All of these parts can be replaced, of course, but it would be better to get rid of the old car and buy a new one.

This is precisely what Paul calls his "strange and wonderful secret." He goes on to say that "we shall all be given *new* bodies." That is a more desirable and permanent solution than merely replacing worn-out parts. The entire chapter 15 of 1 Corinthians deals with this amazing phenomenon called the new body. Paul had been speaking of the necessity of the Resurrection and its importance to the Christian faith. Then he astounded everyone by revealing that the body that is to be raised will not be the old body patched up, but a brand new one.

After raising the questions: "How will the dead be brought back to life again?" and "What kind of bodies will they have?" (1 Cor. 15:35), Paul makes some interesting comments. The new bodies will be different from the old in that they will never suffer sickness, disease or death. Furthermore, "All who become Christ's will have the same kind of body as his" (v. 48). No one knows for certain what the new body will consist of, for he says it will be a spiritual body. But it is sufficient to know that "when he [Jesus] comes we will be like him" (1 John 3:2).

No wonder Paul calls this a "strange and wonderful secret." It is still a secret to the world, but it is now a revealed truth for the believer. So, when we become concerned about this old body, we can console ourselves with the truth that we will someday trade it in for a new one.

Prayer
Lord Jesus, your Church has been waiting many centuries for that last trumpet call announcing your return. Thank you for giving us a hope that goes beyond this painful world. Each day we look forward to your coming. Amen.

TASSELS, BLUE HEMS, AND COMMANDMENTS

The Lord said to Moses, "Tell the people of Israel to make tassels for the hems of their clothes . . . and to attach the tassels to their clothes with a blue cord. The purpose of this regulation is to remind you, whenever you notice the tassels, of the commandments of the Lord." Numbers 15:37-39

FORGETFULNESS is not the exclusive privilege of the retired person. It is a malady common to all ages. We all have our own ways of trying to overcome it. Some write memos to themselves, some try to remember things by association, and a few still believe in tying a string around a finger. My trouble is, I forget where I put the memos, I can't recall the association word, and I fail to remember what the string was there for.

God is familiar with this human weakness, for he has constantly given us visible symbols to aid us in remembering. The celebration of the Lord's Supper is an outstanding example of this truth. "Do this in remembrance of me," said Jesus. Thus the communion service is a regular reminder to us of Christ's sacrifice for our sins.

In Numbers 15 we read about another example of God's many reminders. God said, "I want all Hebrews to wear tassels on their outer clothing, fastened around the hem with a blue cord." Each morning as the people donned their garments, the tassels reminded them of their commitment to keep the commandments of the Lord.

Unfortunately, as time went on, many Hebrews flaunted their tassels and blue bordered hems as a sign of their spirituality. They felt that by widening this blue border they were even more pious. This custom was still in vogue when Jesus came, and he condemned the broadening of their hems as hypocrisy (see Matt. 23:5).

People had also begun to attach superstitious powers to these blue hems. In Matthew 9:19-22 we read about the anemic woman who pressed through the crowd, hoping that by touching the hem of Christ's garment she would be healed. Jesus healed her, not because she touched his garment, but because of her faith.

Today we have no such clothing regulation to remind us to keep the law. But God's law is written upon our hearts. We also have access to his written Word. If we read it each day, we will be reminded anew of our commitment to Christ.

Prayer
Dear Father, thank you for the many reminders of your loving concern for us. It is proof that you want to keep us from suffering the sad consequences of breaking your commandments. Amen.

TIME TO REST

"Come to me and I will give you rest—all of you who work so hard beneath a heavy yoke."
Matthew 11:28

WE were at a nice restaurant with another retired couple, and had just started to look at our menus when the young waiter said with a smile, "You are just in time, we have extended the 'happy hour' another twenty minutes." My friend responded, "Son, when you get as old as I am, the 'happy hour' is an afternoon nap."

None of us cares to admit it, but we find ourselves requiring more rest as we keep adding birthdays. However, we are not alone in this need, for in this hectic, tumultuous world, everyone needs to lie down occasionally, blot out distractions, and relax for a while.

Jesus recognized this need for rest. His disciples had just returned from an exhausting preaching mission. They were tired and weary, for they had been ministering to the masses of people, binding up their wounds, listening to their problems, and telling people about the love of Christ. After listening to their report, Jesus said, "Let's get away from the crowds for a while and rest" (Mark 6:31).

But there is an even greater need than the need for physical rest. In Matthew 11 we see Jesus speaking to a crowd of cynics and calling down the judgment of God upon their cities. Then he concluded his remarks with a loving invitation, "Come to me and I will give you rest—all you who work so hard beneath a heavy yoke" (Matt. 11:28)

The people to whom Christ spoke were indeed burdened with a heavy yoke. Burdens were imposed upon them by a corrupt political system. There were social and economic burdens that weighed heavily upon them. And there were religious burdens caused by a multitude of restrictions and petty requirements. Jesus accused the religious leaders of laying burdens upon the people that neither they nor their ancestors were able to bear. Recognizing the people's weariness and hopelessness he offered to meet their needs.

To all who want to be free of their load of sin and guilt and enjoy true spiritual rest Jesus says, "Come to me." And to all who respond to his invitation, the Bible promises "a place of rest." "We who believe God can enter into his place of rest. . . . So there is a full complete rest *still waiting* for the people of God" (Heb. 4:3, 9). What a happy prospect!

Prayer

Father, thank you for lifting my burden of sin and guilt, and giving me rest. I have learned that this world is no place for rest, for it is ceaselessly on the move. I long for the fulfillment of your promise for eternal rest. Amen.

 # DO I HAVE TO BE ON TOP ALL THE TIME?

Pity me, O Lord, for I am weak. Heal me, for my body is sick, and I am upset and disturbed. My mind is filled with apprehension and with gloom. Oh, restore me soon. Psalm 6:2, 3

AN elderly church member, living in a nursing home, seemed unusually depressed on one of my visits. She burst into tears and said, "Pastor, I know that as a Christian I should be strong spiritually, but do I have to be on top of things *all* the time?" I explained to her that no one who ever lived was on top all the time. Some of the greatest Christians in the world experienced low times. D.L. Moody, Martin Luther, Jonathan Edwards, and many other dynamic Christian leaders have written about their spiritual highs and lows.

It is the nature of humanity to experience times of spiritual discouragement. David wasn't always on top. Physical sickness had weakened his body and caused him to become depressed and disturbed when he wrote, "Pity me, O Lord. . . . Heal me. . . . Oh, restore me soon" (Ps. 6:2, 3). It happens to all of us. There is a natural and necessary letdown at times that is essential for our physical, emotional and spiritual well-being. Batteries run down and need recharging. Fires die down and need rekindling. Physical bodies run down and need rest. And Christians need to come down from the mountaintop experience, unwind and be restored.

As a matter of fact, it is unnatural, if not dangerous, for a Christian to continue on a spiritual and emotional high all his life. There is a natural ebb and flow that is not only healthy, but necessary. During our low periods it is important for us to rest on the encouraging promises of God's Word, to keep in touch with a friend or neighbor, and to enjoy something of God's creation—if nothing more than a single flower or tree.

No, God doesn't expect you to be on top *all* the time. Sometimes the best medicine is simply a week's vacation.

Prayer

Lord, make me aware of my own humanity. Help me to know the difference between physical weakness and spiritual weariness. Remove the feeling of guilt, and revive my anxious heart. Amen.

Musings . . .

There is nothing the body suffers that the soul may not profit by. George Meredith

HE GIVETH MORE
He giveth more grace when the burdens grow
* greater,*
He sendeth more strength when the labors
* increase;*
To added affliction He addeth His mercy,
To multiplied trials, His multiplied peace.

When we have exhausted our store of endurance,
When our strength has failed ere the day is half
* done,*
When we reach the end of our hoarded resources,
Our Father's full giving is only begun.

His love has no limit, His grace has no measure,
His power no boundary known unto man;
For out of His infinite riches in Jesus
He giveth and giveth and giveth again.
Annie Johnson Flint

All things must change—but God remains.
Mary Augusta Ward

Personal soundness is not an absence of problems,
but a way of reacting to them.
Donald W. Mackinnon

Fear not that your life shall come to an end, but rather that it shall never have a beginning.
John Henry Newman

Age is a quality of mind;
If you've left your dreams behind,
If hope is cold,
If you no longer look ahead,
If your ambitious fires are dead,
Then you're old!
Anonymous

The great man is he who does not lose his child's heart. Mencius

Let your old age be childlike, and your childhood like old age; that is, so that neither may your wisdom be with pride, nor your humility without wisdom. St. Augustine

Most of us spend a lot of time dreaming of the future, never realizing that a little of it arrives each day. Author Unknown

Books Worth Reading . . .

Libraries and bookstores are favorite haunts for retired people. Now that you have time to read, here are a few good books you will want to include in your reading adventures.

This is not a comprehensive list. Instead, it is a grouping of titles and book descriptions—samples to whet your reading appetite.

LIVING AND GROWING AS A CHRISTIAN

. . . new books and older books that deal with the joys and challenges of Christian living.

Seasons of Life, To Understand Each Other, and *The Gift of Feeling* by Paul Tournier (John Knox)

Paul Tournier, a noted Swiss physician and counselor, has made a significant contribution to our understanding of psychology and its relation to the Christian faith.

Tournier now lives in active retirement in the small Swiss village where for nearly fifty years he was doctor and counselor. *The Gift of Feeling* was written a few years ago when the author was eighty. This book is partially autobiographical as Tournier tells something of his early life and shares from the life he had with his wife, Nelly. These books, along with Tournier's *Healing of Persons,* are valuable reading.

The Positive Power of Jesus Christ by Norman Vincent Peale (Living Books, Tyndale)

"When one has written twenty-four books it would seem that is enough," says Norman Vincent Peale. Then he explains his desire to write a book describing changed lives through faith in Jesus Christ. *The Positive Power of Jesus Christ,* written when Dr. Peale was past eighty, is that book—a page-by-page revelation of Christ's power at work today in lives committed to him.

Living under the Smile of God by Roger D. Palms (Tyndale)

An invitation to discover the warmth of God's love, the sunshine of his smile as you sense God's pleasure in you—his creation and his child. An inspirational book reminding the reader of God's presence in everyday life.

The Fight by John White (InterVarsity Press)

There is joy and triumph in the Christian life. But as Christians new and old know, joy is often intertwined with struggle. John White takes the reader through basic areas of Christian living where we all wrestle with faith, prayer, temptation, guidance, fellowship and work. Refreshing insights into the struggles and joys of living with Christ.

Loving God by Charles Colson (A Judith Markhan Book, Zondervan)

A book that zeroes in on how to grow as a Christian. Colson deals with many passages of Scripture in terms of Christians showing love to God through their lives. "Most of us don't really know how to love God . . . ," he observes. And "We haven't given thought to what the greatest commandment means . . . and we haven't obeyed it. . . ." This is not a book to encourage you to get more out of your Christianity. Instead it deals with what more you can put into your relationship with God.

How to Be a Christian without Being Religious by Fritz Ridenour (Regal)

Excerpts from Romans, contemporary commentary, and thought-provoking cartoons combine to make this a valuable handbook on how to be a Christian without the burdens of being religious.

If that sounds like a contradiction, let the author clarify the difference in striving to be religious and responding to all God has done for you. "The Christian life," says Ridenour, "is a relationship with God, not a religious treadmill."

Fearfully and Wonderfully Made and **In His Image** by Paul Brand and Philip Yancey (Zondervan)

Fearfully and Wonderfully Made deals with insights into spiritual realities through the eyes of Dr. Brand, a surgeon, as he sees the similarities of a healthy spiritual and physical life.

In His Image again uses likenesses in the spiritual and physical as they focus on the community of Christians referred to in the New Testament as Christ's Body.

Yancey, a fine writer, and Brand, a world-known hand surgeon, make an excellent team to challenge the reader's thinking and spirit.

Making All Things New by Henri J. M. Nouwen (Harper & Row)

In the introduction of this small book, Henri Nouwen explains, "I would like to explore what it means to live a spiritual life and how to live it." He has divided his reflections on the spiritual life into three parts. The first discusses the destructive effects of worry; the second shows how Jesus responds to our worries; and the third describes specific disciplines which can cause our worries to slowly lose their grip on us, and thus allow the Spirit of God to do his recreating work.

A book that inspires the reader to seek times with God.

Living on the Ragged Edge by Charles R. Swindoll (Word)

If you've ever experienced anxiety, stress, money problems, or physical difficulties you will welcome the good news Swindoll uncovers as he explores Ecclesiastes. Take a look at Solomon in his search for pleasure. What did he discover? *Living on the Ragged Edge* offers calmness and strength to replace stress.

Forgive and Forget by Lewis B. Smedes (Harper & Row)

Smedes presents forgiveness as the only way to heal the hurts of life. He says, "The only way to heal the pain that will not heal itself is to forgive the person who hurt you. Forgiving stops the rerun of the pain. . . ." A book that offers specific steps for understanding how to forgive and the importance of forgiveness in every person's life.

Why Waste Your Illness? by Mildred Tengbom (Augsburg)

An encouraging, Bible-centered approach to dealing with pain, loneliness, and frustration. The author offers practical ways to dispel fears, make adjustments, change relationships, and best of all—how to let God use the difficulties of illness for growth and good.

BIOGRAPHIES

. . . getting better acquainted with great men and women of faith.

Augustine, Wayward Genius by David Bentley-Taylor (Baker)

The story of Augustine's life (A.D. 354–430) is much like a brilliant meteor flashing across early Christian history. After resisting Christianity until he was over thirty, Augustine dedicated his many talents to serving Christ as pastor, bishop, writer, statesman, scientist, and world traveler.

Faith's Heroes by Sherwood E. Wirt (Cornerstone Books)
Names of heroes of the faith you've heard all your life come alive in this beautifully written collection of profiles. Polycarp, Vibia Perpetua, Augustine, Francis of Assisi, Martin Luther, Ulrich Zwingli, John Calvin, George Fox, George Whitefield, and Amy Carmichael become people—fellow Christians—individuals you care about.

C. H. Spurgeon by Arnold Dallimore (Moody Press)
A new biography of Spurgeon's life that reveals the great preacher as a learned theologian, a man of prayer, a loving father and husband, and a human being who often knew discouragement and ill health. A touching and powerful look at Spurgeon, the "prince of preachers."

To All the Nations: The Billy Graham Story by John Pollock (Harper & Row)
The master biographer, Pollock, helps the reader see and understand the evangelist Billy Graham and his worldwide ministry that has stretched over the past four decades. A fascinating picture of a remarkable man and his work.

Charles Finney by Basil Miller (Bethany House)
D. L. Moody by Faith Coxe Bailey (Moody Press)
The stories of the lives of these two Christian giants

of evangelism give an inspiring account of men who won thousands to Christ. You cannot read these books without feeling the power and dedication of these two great preachers.

George Muller of Bristol by Arthur T. Pierson
Mary Slessor of Calabar by W. P. Livingstone
(Clarion Classics, Zondervan)

Does your prayer life need the story of a man of almost unbelievable faith? Would you like to step into the life of a missionary whose faith and commitment will amaze you? These biographies of God's servants challenge and revive today's Christian.

Martin Luther Had a Wife and **C. S. Lewis Had a Wife** by William J. Petersen (Living Books, Tyndale House)

While not complete biographies these carefully researched and well-written books give heartwarming glimpses into the family life of great Christian leaders. Famous names become people as you discover their marriages were not necessarily great marriages. Just like the rest of us they faced everyday sorts of problems.

The Luther book includes chapters that enable you to have a glimpse not only into the life of the Luthers, but also into the homes of the Wesleys, the Edwards, the Moodys and the Booths.

The Lewis book includes chapters about the Knoxes, the Hudson Taylors, Billy and Nell Sunday, along with Frank and Grace Livingston Hill.

CLASSICS
. . . books to read again and again, exploring for new discoveries.

Christian Classics and **Famous Prayers** compiled by Veronica Zundel (Eerdmans)

Two beautiful collections. *Christian Classics* is a collection of brief extracts from the works of over sixty Christian authors from the first century to the present day. Many different viewpoints and traditions are represented but all of the writers were inspired by their love of God and belief in Jesus as Savior of the world. Short biographies and illustrations set the authors in the context of their times.

Famous Prayers is a gathering of over 100 prayers offered by Christians throughout the history of the church. The selections are arranged chronologically and annotated with biographical and background information.

The Christian's Secret of a Happy Life by Hannah Whitall Smith (Revell, also Word)

More than 2 million copies of Mrs. Smith's classic have been sold since the book was first published in 1870. Two publishers offer the book with guides for study. The Revell edition includes a passage from the book along with a Bible verse and prayer for each day of the year. The edition from Word includes a study guide written by Elisabeth Elliot.

The Answers of Jesus to Job by G. Campbell Morgan (Baker)

When Job faced his problems and troubles in ancient times he did not have the teachings of Jesus to answer his questions and to provide comfort, assurance, and peace. This older book that examines Job's cries for help, in light of our rich resources in Christ, is a book of encouragement and strength.

The Inner Life by Andrew Murray (Clarion Classics, Zondervan)
The Prayer Life by Andrew Murray (Moody Press)
In His Steps by Charles M. Sheldon (Chosen Classics, Chosen)
Choice Notes from the Psalms by F. B. Meyer (Kregel Publication)

Publishers do today's readers a great service to reprint these valuable Christian classics. Read or reread these books for insights concerning Scripture and God's presence in our everyday lives.

HISTORY COMES ALIVE

. . . books that tie today's faith to the realism of human history, archeology, and geography.

Treasures from Bible Times by Alan Millard (Lion Publishers)

Visually exciting pictures as well as the informative commentary bring to light discoveries that enhance Bible study.

The Archeology of the New Testament by E. M. Blaiklock (Thomas Nelson)

Focused on the life and times of the early church, Blaiklock's explanations of archeological artifacts reveal the world of the early Christian that "in many ways was not very different from the world of today, anxious, war-ridden, disillusioned." Provides powerful evidence of the lives of the early Christian world.

The Old Testament and the Archaeologist by H.D. Lance (Fortress)

H.D. Lance sees archaeology as an aid to understanding the Bible and in this readable book explains his views of biblical archaeology. This is a good book for the person with a limited knowledge of archaeology. Lance provides a good background for understanding as he explains both the values and limitations of archaeology.

101 Hymn Stories by Kenneth W. Osbeck (Kregel Publications)
A Hymn Companion by Frank Colquohoun (Morehouse Barlow)

Who were the people who wrote the words to our favorite hymns? How was the music composed? What were the human stories behind the hymns? Where were the hymns first sung?

These two well-researched books are filled with factual information about the writers, dates and sources of many of the well-known hymns.

Martyrs of Our Time by William Purcell (CBP Press)

All of the martyrdoms described in this thoughtful book took place in the twentieth century, many since World War II. The martyrs include John and Betty Stam, 1934; and Dietrich Bonhoeffer, 1944; and more than two dozen others including the thirteen members of the Elim Pentecostal Church who died in Zimbabwe on a June night in 1978. These men and women, from all traditions of Christendom, gave their lives rather than disobey God's will as they followed Christ.

FICTION AND NEAR FICTION
. . . stories from the past and present that delight the mind and spirit

Ragman and Other Cries of Faith by Walter Wangerin, Jr. (Harper & Row)

A collection of twenty-six pieces including narrative, fable and autobiography. *Ragman* reflects Wangerin's experiences as a pastor of a small inner-city church in the midwest and reveals his warmth, sensitivity and faith.

The Fisherman's Lady, The Marquis' Secret and ***The Shepherd's Castle*** by George MacDonald (Bethany House)

Mystery, adventure and romance combine in these dramatic stories by George MacDonald, master storyteller of the nineteenth century. Another classic of

MacDonald's retold for contemporary readers is *The Musician's Quest.*

A Trilogy: **The Singer, The Song** and **The Finale** by Calvin Miller (InterVarsity Press)

A retelling of the story of the New Testament. The characters take the readers through myth and fantasy to Truth. Reading Calvin Miller's *Trilogy* is much like taking a journey to a far land that in some almost magical way proves to be close to home.

Hagar, Miriam, Ruth, Abigail, and **Lydia** by Lois T. Henderson (Harper & Row)

Novels of women of the Bible, written by Lois Henderson, are exceptionally good reading. The stories weave drama and history together, with the author taking pains to be true to history and the biblical facts.

Priscilla and Aquila by Lois T. Henderson with Harold Ivan Smith (Harper & Row)

The late Lois Henderson's final novel is the retelling of the New Testament story of Priscilla and Aquila. It is a powerful tale, a skillful blend of facts and imaginative story telling. Harold Ivan Smith completed the writing of this book following Lois Henderson's sudden death.